9 Habits of Highly Effective Teachers

A Practical Guide to Empowerment

Jacquie Turnbull

continuum

Continuum International Publishing Group
The Tower Building, 11 York Road, London SE1 7NX
80 Maiden Lane, Suite 704, New York, NY 10038

British Library Cataloguing-in-Publication Data
A catalogue record for this book is available from the British Library.

ISBN: 0-8264-9121-9 (paperback)

Library of Congress Cataloging-in-Publication Data
A catalog record for this book is available from the Library of Congress.

Typeset by Aarontype Limited, Easton, Bristol
Printed and bound in Great Britain by Ashford Colour Press, Gosport, Hampshire

Contents

List of Figures   vi
Acknowledgements   vii

Introduction: What this book is about and how to use it   1

Part I: Managing Yourself   15
   Habit 1: Thinking for yourself   17
   Habit 2: Laying the foundation of confident performance   34
   Habit 3: Taking action on stress   54
   Habit 4: Taking your time   74

Part II: Engaging with Others   97
   Habit 5: Establishing creative rapport   99
   Habit 6: Attentive listening   117
   Habit 7: Practising the behaviours of influence   133

Part III: Spreading the Influence   151
   Habit 8: Influencing leadership behaviours   153
   Habit 9: Extending the influence   169

Conclusion   188

Appendix 1: Presuppositions of Neuro-Linguistic programming   190
Appendix 2: Unique thinking comfort-zone   193
Bibliography   195
Index   200

List of figures

1	Triangle of balance in service quality	5
2	Neuro-logical levels	24
3	Blind-spot	37
4	The yips	38
5	Sensory acuity: some things to look out for	43
6	Johari window	46
7	Taking action on stress	58
8	Balloon and the basket	66
9	'Einstein's dreams'	76
10	Urgent/important matrix 1	84
11	Urgent/important matrix 2	86
12	Thinking processes	102
13	Creating rapport by body-matching	104
14	Creating rapport by matching language patterns	109
15	Visual recall	123
16	Being assertive	137
17	Receiving criticism	142
18	The group process	157
19	Being entrepreneurial	177

Acknowledgements

Writing this book has reminded me of the old metaphor concerning the plumber and a hammer. The story goes that this plumber asked for £50 for work that entailed tapping a pipe with a hammer. When the customer queried the price, the plumber submitted a more detailed invoice:

For tapping the pipe with a hammer	£5
For knowing where to tap	£45

While the time taken to write this book has not been long in the scale of things, 'knowing where to tap' has taken a lifetime's experience. It has been an experience acquired over many years of teaching and training, lecturing and learning and being active in the roles of school and college governor and council member for the General Teaching Council for Wales. It's been such a mixed bag of educational experience that I've always felt rather diffident about describing my working life as a 'career'. The term implies some sort of intentional progression which doesn't match with the way I've always been drawn to different experiences. I've often felt that 'patchwork-quilt' is a more apt description for my life in education.

So when it came to wanting to thank all the people who have contributed to 'knowing where to tap', I began to make a list. There were people who over the years had been mentors and by whom I'd been taught and trained. There were colleagues from whom I'd learned valuable lessons and students who had taught me something about learning. There were colleagues who also became friends with whom I could feel comfortable exploring ideas. When it came to writing this book, there were those who read my early drafts and made valuable suggestions for improvements. There were the people I've identified whose experiences provided illustrations of the habits. There were

those who helped with proofreading and the technicalities of produ-
cing diagrams. There was my long-suffering family who put up with
life being on hold and even provided encouragement.

So I came to the conclusion that to name all the people who have
made a contribution would take a chapter in itself, and I would run the
risk of causing offence by leaving someone out. While I have endeav-
oured to be scrupulous in acknowledging sources of information, I
also have to concede that, with so much learned over a long career,
I may well have absorbed aspects into my own learning and forgotten
the original source.

So, dear reader, if you recognize your influence in these pages,
I hope you will include yourself in this general acknowledgement, and
accept my sincere and grateful thanks.

Introduction: What this book is about and how to use it

'The one thing that is certain is that there is a lot of uncertainty about' [1]

Teaching in the twenty-first century

When the first meeting of the General Teaching Council for Wales was held in September 2000, a fellow council member commented: 'Today, we became a profession.' Indeed, for those of us involved on that day, it did feel like a momentous occasion. For the first time, teaching had its own professional body to ensure standards within the profession and promote its status in wider society.

As an occupation, teaching has always carried less weight and influence than the major players in the professional field, such as law and medicine. Alongside nursing and social work, teaching had been categorized a 'semi'-profession, rather than being identified as a group with ownership of special intellectual or scientific knowledge and the position to influence society.[2] And certainly during the latter part of the twentieth-century, teaching has been the focus of more criticism and interference than ever before. In the UK, the past twenty years have seen the introduction of twenty different Education Acts bringing changes, such as the introduction of a national curriculum, which have engendered a continuous stream of prescriptive requirements upon the teaching profession. In England, what could be called a public shaming is enacted when schools fail to measure up to Ofsted inspections and when league-tables as a measure of performance of schools are printed in newspapers.[3] Yet teachers in the UK need not feel unique in this: similar forms of close examination of state schooling are also happening in Australia, the USA and New Zealand.[4]

Teaching is also not alone among the professions in feeling the pressures of public interest and scrutiny. At the beginning of the twenty-first century, all the professions are under a critical public gaze where issues of standards, accountability and quality of service are open to examination.[5] And in teaching we also have to deal with a lingering public perception of what a 'good' education involves, which frequently includes a vision of teachers standing in front of compliant, attentive classes delivering their expert knowledge.

We also have to deal with a knowledge explosion in the twenty-first century. This affects everyone, of course, but for people working in public services there are additional pressures. Firstly, in addition to being asked to work harder, the information revolution brings with it an expectation that we have to be able to master these advances and work smarter as well. Secondly, the free and open access to information from the media and the Internet has raised the general awareness of the public, and this in turn has raised expectations of public services and those who work in them. When these expectations are not met, dissent, disagreement or disillusionment can often be the result.

Changing meanings of 'professionalism'

So despite my colleague's confident assertion at the inaugural meeting of the General Teaching Council for Wales, there remains uncertainty around the 'professional' status of teaching. Indeed, part of that uncertainty concerns the interpretation of the word 'professional' itself. Words change their meaning over time, and this can certainly be recognized in this case. One hundred years ago, to be a professional meant to have status in society, not only by virtue of ownership of a unique body of knowledge but also carrying a moral authority that was recognized and given due deference. Currently, when we may have estate agents referring to themselves as professionals, window-cleaners claiming to provide a professional service and sellers of used cars celebrating a professional code of practice,[6] it is little wonder that the term defies common agreement as to its meaning.[7]

Of course, the 'old' criteria that defined a profession are no longer relevant because the society we live in is very different. With the expansion of the 'knowledge society', a profession can no longer claim a unique and protected body of knowledge. Being able to operate with a high degree of autonomy no longer seems relevant because in a more open society we are required to be more accountable. And a new aspect that did not apply previously is the requirement for continuing professional development.

Teachers currently at the stage of retirement from the profession would have had an initial experience that differed greatly from today's younger teachers. After qualification, their professional development would have been gained from their own experience behind the closed door of their classroom. Contrast this with the experience of a graduate in Wales today. Having attained qualified teacher status, a newly qualified teacher will now have to achieve the induction standards in her first year, followed by two years of supported early professional development. In the twenty-first century, continuous learning and development throughout professional life not only ensures professional development, but is also essential to keep pace with rapid social change and the expansion of knowledge. With estimates that knowledge will double every seven years from now on[8] there can be no other expectation.

Changing society

There can be no doubt that the complexity of life in the twenty-first century, together with ongoing social changes, have impacted upon the professional role of teachers. The range of pressures was described in an important review of initial teacher training: the changing nature of work and knowledge in an 'information society', the impact of ICT, the changing employment structure of schools, the growing recognition of the importance of evidence-based practice and the pressure to raise standards. The authors came to the conclusion: 'What is significant about all these pressures is that they progressively add to the complexity of teaching.'[9]

Social changes have affected every part of life, not just the professional life of teachers. Sociologists have studied the effects of the knowledge explosion on everyday lives, and how changes in family and work roles have led to the emergence of a new and qualitatively distinct form of society. It follows that to be able to negotiate such a fast-changing world in the future, people will need to be creative, to have the ability to respond flexibly to new situations, to find innovative solutions to difficult problems. People will need to adjust flexibly when interacting with others and will need to communicate on an emotional as well as a cognitive plane. To cope with the challenge of twenty-first century society, people will need creative minds and complex selves.[10]

If as teachers we are to prepare future society for these challenges, we will need to be up to the challenge ourselves. We will need to develop our capacity to work stress-free in a complex, exacting environment. We will need to maximize our personal and professional development. We will need to develop the skills of working with a range of other professionals in order to maximize the potential of those who depend upon our professional ability.

How the habits fit with professional development

The habits described in this book are therefore where I believe we should start in building a 'new' professionalism appropriate for the twenty-first century. They are aspects of personal development that form a solid base for the development of professional expertise. If we are to meet the challenges before us, we will need to learn to work 'effectively, openly and authoritatively' with a range of partners.[11] To do that, we need to build a repertoire of skills and abilities so we can be the leading learners in our society.

At whatever stage of their teaching career, all teachers will have a code of conduct and professional standards to provide guidelines for their professional practice. This book is not seeking to duplicate these or cut across them in any way. Rather it is about the 'how to': how to develop the thinking and behaviours that will enable you to achieve the required professional standards.

This book is also not about the activities of teaching as such, although the illustrations and examples are all based on teachers and their approach to their role. There are many books on how to teach, and this is not one of them. However, you can't of course separate your personal development completely from your teaching role. So the learning you acquire from this book will inevitably impact upon your teaching. Just as the paradigm of pedagogy is shifting from *teaching* to *facilitating learning*, so you will find improved relationship skills will shift your focus in your role as an educator. A shift that involves moving from being a *sage on the stage* to *a guide on the side*.[12]

Another way of considering the relationship between the personal focus of this book and the professional expertise of a teacher, is illustrated in Figure 1. Researchers into quality in public sector work have suggested that service quality can be defined by three components.

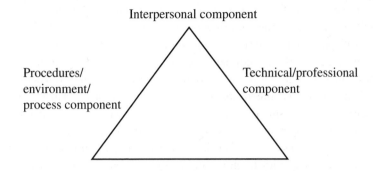

Interpersonal component

Procedures/
environment/
process component

Technical/professional
component

Figure 1 The triangle of balance in service quality
Source: Morgan and Muryatroyd 1994. (Reproduced with kind permission of the Open University Press/McGraw-Hill Publishing Company.)

The three aspects of quality can be seen in different perceptions of the professionalism of a teacher, as demonstrated in interviews with school-children. When asked the reasons why they learn more with some teachers than others, some responded 'they are willing to help you individually' (interpersonal); others said 'they really know their subject' (technical) and yet others thought 'there is control, you know what you are supposed to do' (procedures/environment). Yet the important point is that the triangle is equilateral, and the model assumes a balance between the three types of component for the delivery of a good professional service.[13]

An expression of values

Inevitably there are values of my own that underpin the practical advice in this book. The experience of many years of training in self-development and interpersonal skills, of teaching and of research, have all led me to the same conclusion: that the 'personal' element of work is crucial to overall work-satisfaction and achievement. I can relate to the analysis of the philosopher who suggests that as human beings we enter into two basic kinds of relationship with each other: the functional (which has a purpose such as our work) and the personal (which has no purpose other than to enable us to be ourselves). Both are necessary, but the most important point is that the personal is the more important of the two: 'an economic efficiency which is achieved at the expense of the personal life is self-condemned, and in the end self-frustrating ... the economic is for the sake of the personal'.[14]

Of course, while our personal relationships may be the most important, we need the functional – our work-life – for the personal to become real. Yet that is not to say that the organization of our work-life needs to become more important than personal relationships. Rather than focusing on what makes educational institutions effective and how to improve them, we need to be thinking about schools as *person-centred communities*. This is evident from research that makes it clear that for quality teaching and learning, a balance is required in the classroom – a balance between positive social relationships, control and order with a sense of purpose and wide-ranging teaching skills for presenting, explaining and delivering learning activities.[15] Note that this is a balance that depends upon the personal development and interpersonal skills of the teacher. Thus instead of aiming for high-performance organizations, teaching should be understood and practised as a personal and not a technical activity.[16]

It's not just in education that the emphasis is shifting away from improving the performance of organizations – or performativity. Just as the old idea of 'professional' no longer applies, ideas about organizations needing to be structured and efficiency-driven no longer apply. As Gareth Morgan (a writer on organizational behaviour) has highlighted: 'We are leaving the age of organised organisations and moving into an era where the ability to understand, facilitate, and encourage processes of self-organisation has become a key competence.'[17] But although I'm emphasizing the personal element of professional practice, it doesn't mean I'm advocating a return to the more '*laissez-faire*' aspects of 'progressive' educationalists of the 1970s.[18] On the contrary, I believe the approach I am advocating is challenging and will demand an investment of time and effort. But it is an investment in personal development that will result in a 'professionalism' appropriate for the complex and fast-moving times in which we live. It's an attempt to examine the detail of teacher professionalism in positive and principled ways that are flexible, wide-ranging and inclusive in nature.[19] And it is vastly preferable to the alternative, which is seeing teachers reduced to technicians. As an alternative, that would be about being reduced to 'teaching by numbers', or delivering someone else's predesigned, carefully scripted and precisely timed packages, guidelines and assessments.[20] Or, as another writer has put it, reducing teachers to karaoke singers, learning only to follow the bouncing ball of the script.[21]

So the fundamental values that underpin this book relate to personal development and enhanced interpersonal skills being the starting-point for a new, *empowered* professionalism. The book is not about theories or philosophy, rather it is intended to be a very practical guide for all teachers who want their working life to be more than acting as agents of policy. It's an approach to reflective practice that advocates working on aspects of self-development as a means of developing our teaching professionalism. As such, it's a 'both–and'[22] approach that suggests we can develop ourselves personally and in our relationships with others *and* achieve educational goals and targets. It's an approach to professional characteristics that highlights the microskills that augment effective performance.

It is also a challenge to teachers to look beyond subject disciplines and basic pedagogical principles. There are invigorating insights that can be gained from research into how the brain works, how people learn and think. A great deal can be learned by drawing on models such as neuro-linguistic programming, brain-based learning, Brain Gym, emotional intelligence. If teaching can ever make claim to be *the* core profession, then teachers need to embrace advances in knowledge and develop a portfolio of skills to fulfil their role as key agents of change in today's knowledge society.[23] Because highly effective teachers model learning they stimulate learning in others. They take full advantage of learning and communication practices. And in addition to the intellectual and cognitive domains, highly effective teachers are exceptionally strong in emotional intelligence.[24]

How to use this book

So to the habits – the areas of skill and awareness development that form the building blocks of professionalism. I've grouped them into three parts, each one building on the other:

Part I is about managing yourself. Perhaps not surprisingly in a book about personal development it is the largest part of the book. **Habit 1: Thinking for yourself**, encourages you to think about what teaching means for you and how you think about yourself as a teacher. It introduces you to the issue of thinking itself – the amazing potential of our brains, and how to use your unique thinking-style to maximize your potential.

Habit 2: Laying the foundation of confident performance focuses on expanding your ability to see more, hear more and feel more. It's about gaining confidence in your own intuitive judgement and developing a behavioural flexibility to allow you to respond creatively to different situations.

Habit 3: Taking action on stress aims to help you to deal constructively with the unresolved and accumulated mental and physical tension that inevitably accompanies a high-level, stress-inducing occupation. It is an essential insurance against the damaging long-term effects of negative stress.

Habit 4 is also influential in managing stress. **Taking your time** helps you to see how your personal understanding of time impacts upon your ability to manage your workload effectively. Further than that, it's an important habit in order to achieve the work–life balance that is essential to good health and happiness.

Part II moves from a focus on yourself to developing the habits of engaging with others. The basis of good relationships is being able to establish rapport with others, and **Habit 5: Establishing creative rapport** is about just that. Using the knowledge and confidence gained in developing **Habit 2**, you will be able creatively to establish **Habit 5** and lay the groundwork of productive relationships. And since one of the biggest barriers to good communication – if not *the* biggest barrier – is bad listening behaviour, **Habit 6: Attentive listening** takes a sharp focus on how to build a practice of good listening.

Habits 5 and **6** lay the groundwork for **Habit 7: Practising the behaviours of influence**. When you are able to establish good working relationships with other people by building rapport and listening, you will gain their trust and respect. You will gain the confidence from this to be able to express your thoughts and feelings clearly in a manner that can be understood by others – and being able to say 'no'.

Part III invites you to move outside the narrow confines or your classroom, and develop a 'vision' of how your developing teacher professionalism can impact upon wider spheres of influence. **Habit 8: Influencing leadership behaviour** deals with the knowledge, skills and attitudes to become influential in your local working environment. It's about building the capacity to work with other professionals, and with other people and organizations that interact with your professional role. **Habit 9: Extending the influence** takes this further by advocating a role for teachers as *activist* professionals: influencing the development of policy and building democratic learning environments.

You can read the book from the beginning or, depending upon your interest, you can choose to start at a section that has particular relevance for you. But as you can see, the book has been constructed as it is because the skills and attitudes build upon each other. For me, the place to start first is with yourself: your values concerning your work and your self-management skills. This is the foundation upon which to build the skills of good relationships and influence in the following sections.

Towards an empowered profession

Given the recent history of the teaching profession, it is not surprising that teachers and teacher-educators have been preoccupied with issues of short-term survival in the face of an unrelenting flow of new initiatives and inspections.[25] It may also appear that the work of teachers has become *de-professionalized* due to the application of managerialist policies aimed at increasing public accountability of teachers individually and collectively.[26]

Others, however, argue that professions in general are changing, with teaching becoming *more* professional, and that evidence of this can be seen across the world. They maintain that

> occupations such as teaching are becoming more professional, new skills are required, achieving good relationships with client and other stakeholders becomes more important, a more extensive knowledge base has to be mastered and more complex decisions need to be made. Rather than being deprofessionalized, it could be argued that teaching is being reprofessionalized although the new professionalism is different from the mythical professionalism of forty years ago.[27]

And of course there is an element of choice in all things. We have a choice whether to fill our time by engaging in busy work, or by investing in our personal development. If we invest in our personal development we will empower ourselves personally and professionally. And if we do this, we will be able to empower others. We need to recognize both our own role and the role of the profession in contributing to the broad social agenda of educating future citizens, and to use the skills of influence in order to engage a range of stakeholders in education.

If we want to influence the future, the place to start is with ourselves. Developing the habits of highly effective teachers will lay the groundwork for a satisfying and influential career as an empowered professional.

Reflection: What's important to you about teaching?

The first thing you need in approaching this exercise is a quiet place and time to dedicate reflective thought to the questions. In Part 1 you'll find that the words come quickly to you at first, then more slowly. You should be able to come up with seven to nine words, and it's most important that you allow yourself time for words to emerge.

As you add each word, repeat the whole list over to yourself, then ask yourself 'What *else* is important to me about teaching?'

When you think there's nothing else to add, as a double-check ask yourself 'Is there *anything else* that's important to me about teaching?'

Then move on to Part 2.

Part 1

In a single word, what's important to you about teaching?

. . . .

. . . .

. . . .

And what else is important to you about teaching?

. . . .

. . . .

. . . .

And what else?

. . . .

. . . .

. . . .

Is there anything else that's important to you about teaching?

. . . .

. . . .

Part 2

If you were only allowed to have *one* of the things that are important to you about teaching, which would you choose?

. . . .

And if you were allowed to have *one more* thing that's important to you about teaching, which would you choose?

. . . .

And if you were allowed to have *another* of the things that are important to you about teaching, which would it be?

. . . .

Which would be the *next* thing you would choose from the things that are important to you about teaching?

. . . .

And the *next*?   . . . .

And the *next*?   . . . .

What would come *next*?   . . . .

And *next*?   . . . .

Which would be your final choice?   . . . .

. . . .

Part 3

Think about your two lists of the things that are important to you about teaching.

Is there a difference in the order?

Where did the first one you chose in Part 2 occur in your list in Part 1?

And the second, where did that occur in Part 1?

Were there any surprises for you in your choices in Part 2?

If there's a difference in the order between Part 1 and Part 2, has that made you think any differently about yourself and teaching?

In what ways have you thought differently about what's important to you about teaching as a result of doing this exercise?

Notes

1.   Midgley 2002.
2.   Etzioni 1969.
3.   Sachs 2003: 12. In Wales, league-tables of school performance are no longer published, and the inspection body, Estyn, has a less censorious ethos.
4.   Ibid.
5.   Ibid., p. 1.
6.   Ibid., p. 1.
7.   Hoyle and John 1995: 1.
8.   McGettrick 2002.
9.   Furlong *et al.* 2006: 21.
10.   Hage and Powers 1992.
11.   Hargreaves 2000.
12.   Hare and Reynolds 2004.
13.   Morgan and Murgatroyd 1994.
14.   Macmurray 1961: 187.
15.   Morgan and Morris 1999: 136.
16.   Fielding, M. (ed.) 2001: 12.
17.   Morgan 1997.
18.   Turnbull 2004.
19.   Hargreaves 2000: 153.
20.   Goodson 2003.
21.   Hargreaves 2003: 58.
22.   *Narrowing the Gap in the Performance of Schools Project: Phase II Primary Schools* 2005: 18.
23.   Hargreaves and Goodson 2003.

24. Brighouse 2005.
25. Whitty 2000: 292.
26. Sachs 2003: 7.
27. McCulloch *et al.* 2000: 110 cited in Sachs 2003: 7.

Part I

Managing Yourself

Habit 1: Thinking for yourself

I always voted at my party's call
And I never thought of thinking for myself at all.[1]

Not surprisingly, **Habit 1** is more about thinking than action. It may need more of an investment in reflection than the other habits that follow. But I make no apologies for that; **Habit 1** lays the ground-work for the development of all the other habits. Action without thought can just be reaction – a mere responding automatically to things that happen to you.

Adopting **Habit 1** means that you are prepared to think about your identity and your professional role, and to be clear about the differ-ence. It's the first habit, because we need to think about ourselves – and the beliefs and values that we hold – to understand how our thinking directs our behaviour.

Habit 1 is also about understanding 'how' we think as well as 'what' we think. We have a brain capacity of unimaginable proportions: a potential that we hardly tap into during our lifetime. We know enough about how our brains work to understand how thought affects our physiology, and we know that we can change our thinking to bring about dramatic changes in our way of life. We also have a 'style' of thinking that is unique and personal to us. Being able to 'think about your thinking' is a feature that will set you apart from the mundane, and enable you to manage effectively the demands of a complex working environment. So **Habit 1: Thinking for yourself** is a starting-point on the path to professional *empowerment*.

Professional 'identity'

Thinking about your *identity* is a good place to start in thinking about yourself as a teaching professional. In this respect, it often seems to me the teaching profession has a love/hate relationship with itself. On the one hand those who recruit on behalf of the profession convey an image of mature and motivated individuals nurturing young minds towards fulfilment of potential, playing a valuable role in society. Yet once a young teacher is inducted into the profession, they quickly become aware of the widespread use of the teachers' prayer: 'Thank God it's Friday!'

There is indeed a paradox about how we view work overall. Work generally takes up about a third of our day. Work is a strange experience in that it provides some of the most intense and satisfying moments, can give a sense of pride and identity, yet is something many of us are glad to avoid. It is because work is so important in terms of the amount of time it takes and the intensity of the effects it produces in our conscious awareness, that it is essential to face up to its ambiguities if we wish to improve our quality of life.[2]

If we haven't thought too deeply about our work, if we fill our time occupying ourselves with busy work, doubts can sometimes hit us unexpectedly. And when they do, it can lead us to question beliefs we hold about ourselves that perhaps we hadn't considered previously.

It's also possible that doubts about our ability to cope can occur when we're in a demanding work-role, like the person speaking here:

> I was like a colander first of all, you know like half the stuff would be falling through the bottom and half of it you'd manage to save 'cos the holes weren't that big . . . I had this massive learning curve at the beginning, and it was really draining, I was absolutely shattered every day just because of the amount of information that was going on . . . it's very anxiety-provoking because, you don't know whether you've said the right thing, you don't know whether you've worn the right thing, you don't know whether you've addressed that person the right way . . . so sometimes you're asking for things and they look horrified . . . but that's just a case of learning on the job.'[3]

You may be able to sympathize with what's being said. You may also be able to relate it to your own experience and feel that the person speaking might be new to teaching. Actually she was a mature, well-qualified and experienced psychiatric nurse who was describing her new job – a job that had taken her out of her comfort-zone of working in a hospital and required her to work in a very different environment.

I recorded the interview with this nurse when I was researching the experience of mental health nurses working in courts. At the time it was a new initiative of the UK government designed to identify people with mental health problems who had committed offences and direct them towards appropriate health services. For the nurses it meant moving from a hospital as a base to a different environment, and being the only health professional working alongside lawyers, probation officers, police and magistrates. All in all, it was a situation outside the normal working experience of a nurse, and it meant working with people who might hold very different views to those of health professionals.

For all the nurses I interviewed this was a very disconcerting experience. At one level they experienced discomfort when their professional knowledge was being challenged. But there was an even deeper discomfort that led to a crisis of confidence in their identities as individuals. The experience prompted self-questioning from one of them: 'it needed questioning, you know, "Are you as good as you are . . . God, you're doing all this and you sound as if you know what you're doing, but do you really?" . . . I'd stopped being a nurse and become something else.'[4]

All these nurses were very well-qualified and experienced in their profession. And yet a dramatic change in their working lives proved so unsettling that it hit right to the heart of their feelings about themselves and their professional ability. You may wonder how this can be. How can working in a different environment, with different people, actually make you question who you are?

It's because our work makes up a large part of how we think of ourselves that we can view it as part of our identity as a person. For instance, consider the two following statements:

- I work as a teacher.
- I am a teacher.

The first phrase suggests a person who experiences teaching as a role in life, perhaps one among many other roles – partner, sibling, son/daughter, friend, sports-coach, etc. The second statement says a lot more. It suggests someone who experiences 'being' a teacher as part of their identity as a person.

It's not a case of a right or wrong answer: rather it's that thinking about how we experience our work can help us understand things when we encounter difficulties. The nurses I interviewed had made considerable personal investment in the role of a nurse, so that when their expertise was isolated and open to challenge, it felt like a personal assault that unsettled their self-confidence.

Indeed, with work as demanding as teaching (or nursing), perhaps it's not surprising that we invest a great deal of ourselves in the occupation. Then when we come up against a challenging situation or problem it may be difficult to take a step back and think about it logically because we have an emotional involvement. It can be like that for people who have invested all their emotional energy and identity in a job, or a relationship, so that when the job or the relationship ends, they can suffer real psychological distress.

Pause for Thought 1

Gemma is very aware of what other people may be thinking about her. She can be walking down a corridor in school, and if the head is approaching her with a serious look on his face she immediately assumes she's upset him in some way. She finds it very difficult to assess whether her work is satisfactory unless she gets feedback from another person. This means she is constantly worrying about whether other teachers are doing better than her. Any advice she is given she tends to take seriously, and treats as an instruction.

Jamie is very confident in his own judgement and opinions. He knows from within himself when he is right and tends to collect information that confirms his own opinion. He tends to treat feedback or instruction from other people as information which he may agree to follow, or not. He finds it difficult to take criticism even when it's constructive, or to listen to and value the opinion of others.

- Where is *your* focus of attention?
- Are you dependent upon the views of others to know your own worth?

- Or are you so convinced in your own opinion that you can ignore the views of other people?
- Can you be flexible in adjusting your focus of attention?
- Would it be *empowering* for you to adjust your style?

Highly effective teachers can make a realistic assessment of their own professional ability. They know which areas they can feel confident about, and can accept advice from more experienced colleagues regarding areas they need to develop. They can take criticism as helpful, rather than a personal attack, because they are clear about the difference between their identity and their professional role.

Professional 'role'

So part of **Habit 1: Thinking for yourself** is being clear about your professional identity and thinking of your work as being 'a role', whether it's that of newly qualified teacher, classroom-teacher, subject-teacher, etc. You'll also find that awareness of the difference features in **Habit 3: Taking action on stress** because it's a crucial factor in building a stress-proofing attitude. I've deliberately not used the phrase 'playing a role' because teaching is a serious business and I don't want to convey the impression that this strategy is trivializing that role in any way. Indeed, when you're 'in role' you can give the activity your utmost attention and energy and 'live it' to the best of your ability.

There is a simple way of defining the difference between identity and role: *identities organize the meaning, whereas roles organize the function.*[5] So your 'professional identity' will include the overarching beliefs and values you hold about yourself, other people and the whole social environment in which you live and work. It's from this personal value-base that you invest meaning into the roles you enact. And it also means that there needs to be a 'fit' between your personal meaning system and your role as a teacher.

Once you are able to make a distinction this way, once you've thought through your beliefs and values in relation to education, teaching and your own professional identity, you can more easily make a decision in relation to challenging issues that may arise. You will be able to decide if an issue comes within the compass of your 'role', and is something that is capable of adjustment by organizing yourself or your work in a different way. You will also be able to judge whether it is something that needs checking against your beliefs and values. Then the question to yourself may be:

- Is this something that I believe is basically wrong when I think about my beliefs about education and teaching? Something where I need to make a stand on a matter of principle?
  or alternatively
- Has this issue arisen because I haven't been acting in accordance with my beliefs and values in my role as a teacher? If I have the courage to act on my beliefs and values could I change this situation?

The best teachers know when to adjust their practice, and have the courage to act on their beliefs and values to change things they recognize are unfair or inequitable.

Pause for Thought 2: Beliefs and values

We all hold beliefs and values about the important things in life. We draw on our early life experiences and on our culture; we may be influenced by people we interact with, by what we have read and seen on television; by the Code of Practice and standards of our profession. All these contribute to the set of beliefs and values that we use as a guide through our work and life.

Our beliefs and values are such an integral part of us that we may not consciously think about them very often. We take them for granted; they're just part of our understanding of the world. But they can be recognized in our behaviour, in the language we use and in the way we deal with people.

Good teachers are clear about their beliefs and values relating to teaching and education. They do not just 'hold' values and beliefs, they constantly check that they are followed through in their professional behaviour and the way they interact with pupils and colleagues. Their beliefs and values give them a firm base from which to challenge inconsistencies and inequities when they occur. Their professional behaviour is congruent because there is a match between beliefs and values.

Here are some of the beliefs held by highly effective teachers:

- Education has a high moral and social purpose as well as training for employment.
- Intelligence can be nurtured through learning, rather than being a fixed trait with everyone having a certain amount.
- Everyone is a unique being, with thinking and learning styles that are individual to them.
- If a child is not learning, the reason is that the teacher has yet to find the key to enable them to learn.
- One of the greatest things a teacher can do for a child is to encourage self-esteem.

Levels of thinking and experiencing

In defining the difference between 'identity' and 'role', we can also consider different *levels* of thinking. Albert Einstein said that you can't solve a problem by using the same kind of thinking that created the problem; you need to use a different sort of thinking. Therefore thinking through different *levels* helps us to analyse a situation or a problem in different ways.

The other aspect of 'thinking about thinking' at different *levels*, is that there is a *hierarchy* of the levels.[6] (See Figure 2). Each level organizes the information on the level below it, and the rules for changing something on one level will differ from those for changing a lower level.

For example, thinking at the level of *environment* would mean using your sense organs to assess whether your classroom is conducive to learning. What do the pupils see when they walk in – is it an interesting, stimulating environment? Could you introduce the power of music to create a mood that encourages learning? What is the overall sense of the place? What changes could you make that would empower you as a professional and your pupils as learners?

Our *behaviour* involves our physical actions and conscious movements. At this level you can think about whether some of your behaviours are simply knee-jerk reactions, habits or rituals: are they

Identity
Your sense of who you are, and how you relate to systems of which you are a part.
So, depending on who you are you have certain beliefs and values.

Beliefs and values
The fundamental judgements you hold about yourself and the world around you, which underpin and direct your behaviour.
And depending on your beliefs and values you choose skills and knowledge to go after in the world.

Capability
The ability to choose and adapt your behaviours in response to a wider range of situations. An intuitive quality that is able to use different behaviours appropriately.
And depending on the skills and knowledge you have, you use certain behaviours.

Behaviour
The basic physical actions through which you interact with your environment and the people in it.
And depending on those certain behaviours you create and influence the environment around you.

Environment
All the factors that make up the external context in which you work.

Figure 2   Neuro-logical levels
Source: Dilts 1990.

actions of your psycho-motor system in response to external stimuli without any reference to your mental map? On the other hand, the level of *capability* involves being able to select and alter behaviour to suit a variety of external conditions. It involves your mental and intellectual capacity to choose and modify your behaviour to suit different situations.

While *capability* involved the cortex, thinking at the level of *beliefs and values* would mean engaging the limbic system in the mid-brain.

This is the part of the brain that is primarily responsible for emotions and feelings, pleasure and attention, and which also deals with our judgements on what is 'true' or valid. So it is not surprising that when we think about *beliefs and values* we can also experience an associated emotional response. As when something that is an expression of a *belief* makes our 'blood boil' or our 'heart pound' or gives us a 'pain in the neck'. As a trainer, I've often observed physical changes in people as a result of thinking about beliefs and values, and delegates can find it very tiring to engage in activities that require this deeper sort of thinking.

Changing something on a lower level could, but would not necessarily, affect the upper levels; but changing something in the upper levels must necessarily change things on the lower levels in order to support higher-level change. *Identity*, for instance, is physiologically related to the immune system, endocrine system and other life-sustaining functions, and therefore changes in our perception of our identity can stimulate changes in our physiology.[7] It's no wonder that when our identity feels threatened it can be for us a profoundly negative experience. But it also means that when we think positively about our identity, it will make us feel differently about ourselves. The changes in our physiology will mean we interact with people differently, which means people will respond to us differently, which means the environment in which we work will be different.

Brain and body are part of the same cybernetic system

As you'll discover with the other habits, there is no cut-off point that separates your brain from your body. Your brain and body form a feedback loop – each affects the other. The recent attention being paid to the quality of school meals is a recognition of the growing awareness of how to feed the body to feed the mind. But it's worth spending a moment to focus on the brain, if only to think about the capacity of thinking power we have available to us.

The average brain is a collection of tissue of staggering complexity – a hundred billion neurons (brain cells) connected by a hundred trillion synapses[8] (the gaps where electrical impulses pass between cells). We have to trust our neuroscientist colleagues and their technological advances on this sort of information; you may find it – as I do – quite difficult to comprehend the capacity indicated by those numbers. I have heard of a metaphor that attempts to convey the capacity of an average brain: the suggestion is that the potential connections between neurons are as many as there are grains of sand on all the beaches in the world. What we can be sure of is that the electrical sparks and chemical exchanges between these cells can accomplish some amazing and perplexing things.[9]

While advances in neuroscience have informed us more fully of the structure of the *brain,* the nature of the *mind* still evades scientific comprehension. Figuring out the exact nature of consciousness and the mechanisms by which it emerges out of collections of neurons is truly an important problem. The mind–brain issue continues to tantalize much more knowledgeable brains than mine,[10] so it's not one with which I intend to engage here. But there are some general issues concerning our mind–brain that are relevant to what follows.

Firstly, with the sort of capacity neuroscientists tell us the average brain consists of, there wouldn't seem to be much doubt that we don't fully utilize all the potential that is available to us. Estimates vary as to how much of our brain capacity we use from as little as 2 per cent to 25 per cent at most.[11]

Secondly, neuroscience is beginning to catch up with psychology in discovering changes in the brain that underlie learning. They can now describe how boundaries between swatches of cortex devoted to different body-parts, talents and physical senses can be adjusted by learning and practice. Learning *is* a change in the brain.[12]

Thirdly, we know that given multisensory stimulation and cognitive challenge connections between neurons can be stimulated and learning enhanced. Thus, rather than thinking of the brain as a computer, it can now be seen as 'a flexible, self-adjusting, ever-changing organism that grows and reshapes itself in response to challenge, with elements that wither through lack of use'.[13] So it is true that if you don't use it, you lose it.

All this means that, whatever our status at present, we have the brain-potential to learn, and as a result we have the capacity to change – to empower ourselves by changing our patterns of thinking and behaviour. Because of the capacity of our brain, we have a mind that has infinite unconscious reserves that we can use as resources – once we gain the confidence to acknowledge them and tap into them. We also have abilities that are unique to us as a species, and which have been crucial to our evolution into the cleverest creatures on the planet.

First, we are aware of our own consciousness. This means we can think about our thinking and our emotions, and reflect on our behaviour. Nowadays there is a lot written about *metacognition*, and how we can develop 'thinking about their thinking' in students to gain self-knowledge and self-management. These are the sort of control processes that are recognized as essential for professionals to cope effectively with a complex modern working environment.

Secondly, in surviving and thriving as a species we have developed abilities to adapt to new environments, new social circumstances, to deal with new challenges – to empower ourselves. The brain's plasticity means we have a capacity for learning, creativity, and therefore for change. We have sufficient brain-potential to be life-long learners – without any fear of using up our mind/brain resources.

What sort of thinker are you?

While we all may have similar brain *capacity,* the way that we *use* our brains may be very different. To start with, the way that we understand the world around us will be different for each one of us. We all carry our own internal 'map' of the world as an interpretation and a guide through the world in which we live.

Philosophers have said 'the map is not the territory'[14] for very good reasons. If I wanted to drive to a part of the country I'd never visited before, I would probably want to study a map of the route before I set off. The map would show me the roads to take and other features of the route. It would not be the terrain itself, but a *re-presentation* of the actual terrain.

So it is with your mental map of the world. As your guide on your journey through life, it is your *re-presentation* of reality. We take the information from our senses – what we *see* around us, what we *hear,* and how things *feel* to us – and construct our own mental map of reality. But there is a major difference between your mental map and a road-map. Your mental map is unique to you, because your perception of the world around you will be different from other people's. You will interpret reality according to your own map – how many times have you experienced a misunderstanding between people because two people 'read' a situation completely differently?

The way we perceive the world around us will be unique to us because it is influenced by our background – our upbringing, our education, our culture and language, our memories. All of these will be personal to us and will influence how we judge our life experiences. And the way we construct our internal reality – the way we organize our thoughts – will also be unique to us.

I'll use an example to show what I mean by this. Just pause for a moment and think about how you would interpret this word:

Beach

Quite apart from the different literal interpretations – sandy beach, pebble beach, beach that stretches for miles, beach of a small cove, wondering whether I meant the verb *to* beach – all of which would be the *content* – there would also be the *process* of how you interpreted 'beach'. You may have *seen* a picture of a particular beach from your memory. You may have been able to *hear* the crashing of waves onto shingle. You may have experienced a particular warm *feeling* associated with a holiday. Or you could have *heard your voice* read the word 'beach', have *felt* the wind on your face, have *tasted* salt, or *smelled* the seaweed. However you interpreted 'beach', you will have been using the three main *representational systems* – mentally you will be either generating pictures (*visual*), or hearing sounds (*auditory*) or having feelings (*kinaesthetic*),[15] or a unique combination of these.

Just as we process information from our senses (what we see, hear, feel) we also use these processes to *re-present* reality mentally for ourselves – this is how we construct conscious thought. In addition there is what is termed *auditory digital,* which describes the process of talking to ourselves. And while we all use all of the systems, for some of us what may have started out as a *tendency* to favour one or other of the forms of thought will have become a preference, and end up being our comfort-zone. We may favour one particular system more than the others, and it becomes our usual pattern of thought-processing.

While discovering our own thinking comfort-zone is important to develop our thinking capacity and *empower* ourselves, the best teachers take it a step further. They recognize that we have a tendency to teach to our own thinking style, because that is the way we ourselves learn best. They recognize that we may talk and interact with others in a way that reflects our own thinking style. Once we become aware that our own way of thinking and learning is unique to us, we are more able to recognize that others have different styles.[16] The best teachers are able to enhance their professionalism by adapting their teaching to meet the needs of students with differing thinking/learning styles, and by developing flexibility in their interaction with others.

Pause for Thought 3: What sort of a thinker are you?

One of the lectures I attended during my early training was on group-leadership behaviour. At one stage during the lecture, the lecturer was explaining a particular theoretical idea. I was having considerable difficulty because I just couldn't grasp what she was saying. As I looked around the rest of the class, I could see all the other trainees nodding sagely and contributing to the discussion. I mentally shrank into my seat, embarrassed to think I was the only one who was struggling to understand. Then the lecturer switched on the overhead projector, and illuminated on the screen was a very simple diagram that explained the idea with a few circles and lines. Just as the screen lit up, it was like a light-bulb switching on in my head – seeing it this way, it was *easy* to understand.

When Nigel is working at home, if he reaches a point when he has wrestled with a mental problem for a while, he will take off for a bike-ride around the countryside where he lives. Even when he's on campus at the university and has to make his way from one lecture room to another, he will never take the shortest route. He will usually find a route that will take him outside the buildings for some fresh air, with enough distance to allow him to stretch his legs. He finds that even a short physical break helps him to think more clearly.

Lisa really struggled with her university course. While she was listening to a lecture she thought she had quite a good understanding. But then she'd look back over her lecture-notes and they didn't seem to mean anything to her. No matter how she tried, she just couldn't seem to retain anything of value from the lectures. She raised this with her personal tutor who came up with a suggestion. Had she thought of taping the lectures? Once Lisa started doing this it made all the difference. It meant she could listen to the lecture as many times as she needed to get things straight in her head.

Ann always has a collection of coloured pens with her at a meeting. She will start with a clean sheet of the type of A4 pad that she likes, and her notes will spread in all directions across the page, linked by lines and circles as she makes connections. She admits she prepares for training very differently now than when she first became a trainer. She will use flip-chart-size paper so she can pin the sheets to the wall of her office, coloured pens of course, and also lots of coloured post-it stickers that can be moved from sheet to sheet if necessary. With the sheets on the wall, she can walk around, talking herself through her ideas to test them.

When you get 'stuck' in your thinking it's sometimes easy to slip into feeling that the root cause must relate to the limits of your own intelligence, particularly when other people you are working with seem to have a ready understanding. It's therefore very reassuring to come to an understanding that what may *really* be the root cause is just the fact that the information, or the way that you are working, are not in a form that suits your thinking preference. Highly effective teachers recognize their own thinking comfort-zone and empower themselves by using strategies that help them think, plan and work more effectively.

As in the examples above, this could mean:

- finding that a diagram, drawing or mind-map can help your understanding
- recognising when a physical break is necessary to regain your concentration
- thinking about how you could use audio-tapes to help you work
- using a variety of resources to organize your planning – coloured pens and paper, post-it stickers.

Conclusion

Habit 1 is about thinking about your thinking. It's being clear about the difference between identity and a role, and being able to establish a clear and confident sense of professional identity, informed by a set of beliefs and values. It is important that you think about your beliefs and values in relation to education, and have the confidence to follow them through in your behaviour in the classroom and elsewhere.

Advances in neuroscience and psychology can inform professional practice. By keeping abreast of these you can facilitate learning both for yourself and others.

Highly effective teachers recognize that knowledge is power, and that self-knowledge brings empowerment. Thinking about how we think can lead to changes in how we act; we can learn to manage our social environment and deal with the challenges our professional lives present. **Habit 1: Thinking for yourself** prepares you for making changes to improve your professionalism.

Reflection: Unique thinking comfort-zone

To find your unique thinking comfort-zone, for each group of three statements tick the one that appeals to you most strongly. (Answer quickly, taking your first reaction. There are no right or wrong answers: you are simply choosing the one you prefer.)

a   Listening to music is one of my favourite pastimes.

b   The colours and layout of my classroom are very impor-
    tant to me.

c   I get fidgety if I have to sit in the same place for very long.

a   I would rather talk something through with someone
    than write a letter.

b   I can always see when a word is spelt wrongly.

c   I rely on my gut-feelings a lot when making judgements.

a   The way a teacher's voice sounds is very important in
    teaching.

b   I become more confident when I look good.

c   I like to get in touch with people I'm working with.

a   It helps me think things through if I talk out loud.

b   I understand better if I have a diagram rather than an
    explanation in words.

c   I only understand things fully when I can do them myself.

a   I can usually determine sincerity by the sound of a per-
    son's voice.

b   I find myself evaluating others on their appearance.

c   I can make a judgement by the way a person shakes hands
    with me.

a   I would rather listen to CDs than read books.
b   I like to watch television and go to the cinema.
c   I prefer outdoor activities.

a   I know exactly how my car should sound when it's running smoothly.
b   I like to see my car looking clean inside and out.
c   I like a car that feels good when I drive it.

a   I like people who are easy to listen to.
b   I enjoy 'people-watching'.
c   I can always sense if things are not right with someone.

a   I would rather have an idea explained to me than read it.
b   I like a speaker to use visual aids when they're explaining something.
c   I like to participate in activities rather than watch.

a   I understand things more easily when I say the words to myself.
b   I am good at finding my way using a map.
c   I exercise because of the way I feel afterwards.

a   I often find myself imitating the way people talk.
b   I make a list of things I need to do each day.
c   I prefer to walk to work if possible.

a   If I have a problem, I like to talk it through with someone else.
b   Mind-mapping is a good technique to help me organize ideas.
c   I prefer to weigh up all the issues before I make a decision.

Count up the number of a's, b's and c's and note them below:

No. of a's: ...
No. of b's: ...
No. of c's: ...

Now go to Appendix 2 to check your unique thinking comfort-zone.

Notes

1. Gilbert and Sullivan, *HMS Pinafore*, Act I.
2. Csikszentmihalyi 1997: 49–50.
3. Turnbull and Beese 2000.
4. Ibid.
5. Castells 1997: 7.
6. Bateson 1972.
7. http://nlpuniversitypress.com
8. Pinker 2002: 42.
9. LeDoux 1998: 22.
10. Dennett 1991.
11. Smith 1996: 15.
12. Pinker 2002: 45.
13. Abbott and Ryan 2000: 21.
14. Korzybski 1933.
15. O'Connor and McDermott 1996.
16. A single-sex school in west London has become a laboratory for kinaesthetic teaching in which book-learning is replaced by activities. The reason is that three years ago the staff tested themselves and found their preferred learning-styles were through words, spoken or written. They then tested the boys and found that a large number learned more effectively by doing things than by traditional 'talk and chalk' methods. Following a staff-training programme, kinaesthetic teaching has been adopted and new members of staff are expected to understand about different learning styles. (Report by Liz Lightfoot, 'Action speaks louder than words when it comes to teaching boys', *Daily Telegraph* 28 December 2005.)

Habit 2: Laying the foundation of confident performance

If you always do what you've always done, you'll always get what you've always had.[1]

'What you need,' I tell students, 'is the F-word ... Flexibility.' With worldwide knowledge doubling every seven years, it's not enough for students to pass through their education accumulating only that; what they need in addition are skills of problem-solving, the ability to seek out information and attitudes to sustain a confident and communicative demeanour. **Habit 2** is about building the behavioural and mental flexibility that is a prerequisite for the development of such skills and attitudes.

Habit 2 is essential for professional empowerment because, as well as preparing pupils for a rapidly changing world, teachers have to work in an environment where change is almost all they can be certain of. Because of all the uncertainty about, it's hardly surprising that our modern world appears to have given rise to a new 'uncertain individual', characterized by greater responsibility and, at the same time, greater vulnerability.[2] This makes it even more important to aim for clarity about *identity*, and to be able to separate *identity* from *behaviour* (see **Habit 1**).

Being clear and confident about your identity means you can use it as a fixed point from which to develop the mental and behavioural flexibility that empowers you to cope with an increasingly complex working environment. Thinking of your identity as *who you are*, and your behaviour as *what you do*, makes it easier to recognize that your behaviour is something you can adapt and change to empower yourself and others.

Developing intuition

In many ways, our education has not particularly prepared us for dealing with the complexity of a professional role in twenty-first-century society. University departments are concerned with taking a rational approach to the acquisition of academic subject knowledge, and not necessarily with the *process* of professional behaviour. Secure subject knowledge is important, but there are many situations where what we can 'know' will be insufficient, and where guessing or blind faith is not desirable: 'We need instead to be able to improvise, to divine what is possible and sense our way forward to what is reasonable. We need to learn to use our impressions, hunches and feelings.'[3]

Part of the 'professionalism' of teaching is the ability to make accurate judgements based on intuition. Other professionals have similar capabilities. Nurses have told me that at some time in their career they have faced a situation where they 'knew' something was not right with a patient – even though all accepted scientific measures, such as temperature and blood pressure, gave an indication of stability. And it was usually the case that their 'instincts' proved to be correct. It can also be the case that teachers with a class of 30 boisterous children will have an awareness of what's happening in every corner of the classroom – even to the extent of apparently being able to 'see' what's going on behind them! Trainers I have worked with will have a 'sense' of the atmosphere amongst a group of delegates which they will use to adapt and modify their training strategy.

The case has certainly been made for intuition in professional development and practice taking its rightful place alongside reason and reflection.[4] Good teachers recognize that gaining confidence in their ability to use intuitive insights is one way to broaden the scope of the professional behaviours they can demonstrate. But if you're a new professional, where do you start in developing this intuitive ability? Is it something that depends on your upbringing, which could explain why some people have it and others have not?[5] Or can it be learned? Do you have to acquire a lengthy experience before you can act on intuitive insights with what can be called 'professional judgement'? Because the test of intuitive action as a valid response to events does depend upon the validity of the judgement. So can we empower ourselves by making professional judgements based on intuitive insights?

If intuition is a 'way of knowing and learning' there are two factors that will lay the groundwork to enable us to develop confidence in our ability to respond intuitively and flexibly to situations: *sensory acuity*, which is a way of knowing, and *feedback*, which is a way of learning.

Sensory acuity

When I was a child, there was a popular party game called 'Hunt the Thimble'. First there would be the party tea with the requisite wobbly jelly and blancmange and fancy cakes to be enjoyed. Then the games would begin. Came the time for 'Hunt the Thimble' and all of the children would be shepherded out of the room where we had to wait with mounting excitement. This was the time when the adults inside the room would hide a thimble. An important rule was that the thimble had to be placed somewhere in clear sight. Then the flurry of small bodies tumbled back into the room, and the hunt for the thimble began in earnest. Generally, this was a game that could be relied upon to pass a considerable length of time, because once one of us spotted the thimble we would have to sit quietly and not let on to the others. There would usually be one child who would be last to find the thimble, even when they were standing right in front of it, even despite encouragement from adults on the lines of 'You're cold', 'You're getting warm', 'You're really hot!'

This simple game illustrates how we consciously perceive the world around us. Because of the vast amount of information available to us, we are selective in what we pay attention to (one estimate suggests we have two million pieces of information available to us via our senses at any one time – no wonder we consciously pay attention to only a very small part). So we can focus our attention deliberately, as when we are so focused on a single activity that we filter out all other information about our surroundings. Or, as in the case of 'Hunt the Thimble', it can happen without our intent, when we experience a 'blind spot' that everyone else can see. (See also Figure 3.)

Can we override this 'deletion' facility to enable us to see more, hear more and sense more? Can we 'come to our senses', as the old phrase puts it? We do indeed have the capacity to 'train' our sense organs to a higher degree of expertise – as illustrated in the example of piano-tuners. When apprentice piano-tuners are first instructed to listen to the 'beats' as they strike a key, they are unable to discern anything

As a child I was often taken for country walks. There would often be a whole group of us – uncles, aunts, cousins. On one of these occasions we were heading home along a country lane when one of my cousins urged us to stop. He had spotted a robin perched in a stretch of fencing, just visible through a gap in the hedgerow. Silence fell as the whole group stopped and admired the handsome bird. The whole group, that is, except me, who had no idea what everyone was staring at. 'Look, Jacqueline, look,' whispered my uncle, bending close and pointing at the point in the hedgerow that was transfixing everyone else, 'Look, before he flies away!' I stared and stared, 'Where, where?' I begged. 'There! There!' said my uncle, frustrated now at my lack of response. After what seemed an age during which I peered feeling increasingly stupid, and my uncle pointed with increasing vexation, it was as though a shutter dropped suddenly, and I could see a new picture. There was the bird, in full sight – the bird that everyone else had been able to see all along. Now in clear view, it was no more than five feet away from me – and had been all the time.

Figure 3   Blind Spot

they would describe as a 'beat'. However, if training is successful, they come to be able to isolate the interference 'beats' and notice how the pattern of the beats changes in response to their turning of the hammer on the peg. 'What they typically say . . . is that *their conscious experience has changed*. More specifically, it has been augmented: they are now conscious of things they were not previously conscious of.'[6]

Good teachers gain their apparently intuitive knowledge in a similar way. They may not consciously have trained their sense organs to perceive at an exceptional level. Yet the complexity of our nervous system is so immense that we have the capability unconsciously to register details of our environment. What the nurses in the example above have become experienced at is 'reading' clues such as minute changes in skin colour, muscle-tone or eye-movements. And in taking in the details of a whole classroom, teachers may have expanded the capacity of their peripheral vision so that they have a 'wide-screen' vision of their environment. Yet again, trainers who are sensitive to the 'climate' of a training group may be taking a whole host of clues such as the way people are sitting in relation to each other, body posture, facial expressions, tone of voice, in order to make a judgement on an appropriate training strategy. The fact that these capabilities develop through experience until they operate unconsciously is one reason why professionals find it hard to describe how they do what they do. It's almost as though if they stopped to analyse how they were think-ing what they were thinking, the ability to make an intuitive judge-ment would be hindered (see Figure 4).

Scientists at the Mayo Clinic are studying the 'yips' experienced by golfers. 'Yips' are the delaying tactics exhibited by golfers before they take a putt, when they seem unable to strike the ball, but have to go through an elaborate ritual. The scientists are studying the neurological processes, and think their findings can help in relieving various complaints. First findings indicate that when a golfer has the 'yips' the left side of the brain (analy-tical, logical) is more active.

To golfers of every degree it could be a new golden rule. It is this: golfers were seen to be putting better when the left side of the brain, the analytical side, is quiet and when therefore the motion is taken care of by the right side of the brain, the instinc-tive side.

Most golfers know this in a semi-conscious sort of way, hence the cliché 'paralysis by analysis'.

Famous US golfer Bobby Jones always advocated 'walking up to the ball, one look at the hole – because the brain will have recorded the distance – then strike straight away', i.e. intui-tively, not allowing analytical brain to kick in. Another US golfer, Henry Longhurst, was asked if he ever had the 'yips'. He thought for a while before replying 'No, but I'm a carrier.'

Figure 4   The Yips
Source: Alistair Cooke, *Letter from America*, BBC Radio 4, 27 July 2003.

While we can probably understand how cutting out the analyti-cal component works when putting a golf-ball, teaching is a much more complex activity than a game of golf (although a colleague of mine who is a golf fanatic would probably disagree). Thus while it's becoming acknowledged that the use of intuition is an important aspect of professional practice, there is still a call for intuition to be enhanced by gaining greater critical control over its use.[7] If we really are aiming for flexible behaviour to deal with the complexity of teaching practice, we need to develop a range of 'educated intuitions' to support complex decision-making in the moment.[8]

There's an illustration of how intuitive judgement can develop while still retaining an element of control in the way my strategy for marking essays has developed. When I first became a lecturer, I found assigning a grade to an essay quite a difficult task. I would struggle to analyse objective measures of quality – was the essay well-structured?, did it include all the salient facts?, how well did it answer the question? – then work out a complicated mathematical procedure for assigning a grade. With experience, I developed a different strategy. Nowadays, I read an essay straight through and gain a 'sense' of a grading. Only after that do I check my intuitive assessment by rereading to consider the objective measures, and 99 per cent of the time the objective tests confirm my initial intuitive judgement. Yet it still needs the application of some objective analysis to confirm that my intuitive response has resulted in an appropriate professional judgement.

So to go back to this idea of *sensory acuity* and how we can use it as a critical tool to support the development of intuition. The word 'acuity' is really using an adjective as a noun, but it's rather neater than using 'acuteness'. If you look for some dictionary definitions of 'acute' you will find 'penetrating in perception or insight' or 'sensitive or keen'. Applying these attitudes to what we see, hear and sense means raising our awareness of the information we receive from our senses, and testing the validity of our perceptions so that we can develop an accurate basis for intuitive judgements.

Others have described this process more eloquently. There is a classic book on writing that fascinated me the first time I read it, in which the author describes the practice of shifting from being engrossed in our own personal world to noticing more than we normally notice:

> It is perfectly possible to strip yourself of your preoccupations, to refuse to allow yourself to go about wrapped in a cloak of oblivion day and night, although it is more difficult than one might think to learn to turn one's attention outward again after years of immersion in one's own problems . . . Try to see your home, your family, your

friends, your school or office, with the same eyes that you use away from your own daily route. There are voices you have heard so often that you forget they have a timbre of their own; unless you are morbidly hypersensitive, the chances are that you hardly realize that your best friend has a tendency to use some words so frequently that if you were to write a sentence involving those words anyone who knew him would realize whom you were imitating . . . By the simple means of refusing to let yourself fall into indifference and boredom, you can reach and revive . . . every aspect of your life.[9]

The 'cloak of oblivion' is a neat way of describing how we can be blinded by our personal preoccupations. Since the information from our senses constructs our mental *re*-presentation of the world (see **Habit 1**), we need to be constantly checking the information to ensure our unique mental 'map' is up to date. We need to be alert to the danger that we could be prejudging or stereotyping people and situations because our mental 'map' is stuck in past experience. Intuition develops from experience, but it is only reliable if we are critically aware of that experience to ensure that professional judgements that stem from intuition are soundly based.

This is where awareness of what we are actually perceiving via our senses is so vital. **Habit 2** challenges us to notice what we notice more carefully, and not to make assumptions about what we are seeing, hearing and sensing. We can notice that a person may be red-faced, but if we respond with a behaviour based on an assumption that the person is embarrassed or angry, then we could be making a misjudgement if the person is merely highly sensitive to temperature. It often used to be the case that teenagers I worked with would take grave offence at what they'd interpreted as a 'dirty look' from one of their peers, leading to a confrontation that could quite simply have been avoided.

Pause for Thought 4: Sensory-grounded descriptions

In the following list of descriptions, some are high-quality sensory-grounded observations. Others represent personal metaphors. Some even border on what can be referred to as hallucination. As a handy guide to determine whether a word or phrase is a mind-reading or a description in sensory-based terms, you can ask the question 'How do you know that?'

Place an X next to each statement that is fully described in sensory-grounded language.

1 Her lips thinned and the muscles on her face tightened.

. . .

2 There was a warm expression on his face. . . .

3 It was obvious that she was relieved. . . .

4 I could tell his heart was going a mile a minute. . . .

5 She is pressured by the responsibilities of her job. . . .

6 The tempo of his speech quickened and went up a tone. . . .

7 As you touched him, I could see curiosity all over his face. . . .

8 Suddenly, her breathing was shallow and her chest was hardly moving. . . .

9 As he dilated his pupils, he gazed in total disbelief. . . .

10 As she looked down and right, her face flushed. . . .

11 I could hear the joy in her voice as she spoke. . . .

12 His breathing speeded up as he leaned forward. . . .

13 When she smiled, I knew she was delighted. . . .

14 He took a deep breath and blinked his eyes. . . .

15 His voice sounded louder because he looked excited. . . .

16 As she took a deep breath, her lips thinned. . . .

Source: Stenhouse Consulting.

Sensory acuity also allows us to be switched on to more subtle messages from other people's nonverbal language. We judge a person's meaning as much from their tone of voice as the words they use – being more acutely tuned in to nuances of voice tone and inflection can heighten our sensitivity to whether there is a message underlying the words being said. Judging how to sit or stand in relation to other people can influence a relationship, as can making a judgement over whether touch is appropriate (see **Habit 5**). If you've ever been in a situation where another person has misjudged the distance between you and has intruded into your personal 'comfort-zone', then you'll know how uncomfortable that can be. Sensory acuity means you avoid such misjudgements because you will have a heightened sensitivity to another person's demeanour.

Pause for Thought 5: Same/different

Take three coins of the same denomination and line them up in front of you.

Now ask yourself the question 'What is the relationship between these three?'

How did you respond?

'They're all the same': You are likely to be the sort of person who does not like change, and would prefer things to stay the same. Once you have learned how to do something, you are likely to stick with it. In any new situation you will be looking for something in common with your previous experience. So you would be likely to assess students on their similarities to students you have taught previously.

'They're the same but have some differences': You like things to stay relatively the same but can cope with gradual change. The timetabled structure of the school day and term suits you on the whole; you can accept some changes as long as they don't disrupt the normal routine too much.

'They're different but have some similarities': You like some regularity to your daily work, but mostly have to have some novelty in your working life. You can only cope with teaching the same subject for a number of years by finding new ways of presenting the material.

'They're all different': You thrive on change. You will only be able to stick at the same work long-term if there is enough change to provide you with a challenge. You see every student as being unique and different so are constantly adapting your teaching and looking for innovative ways of presenting material.

Highly effective teachers work within the framework and regularity of school life while being aware of the need to evolve to meet changing circumstances. They are alert to the differences in students and can adapt their teaching methods to meet student needs. Because they recognize that people learn differently, they avoid falling into the trap of teaching in their own preferred learning style. They don't have 'one way' of communicating with other people. They can adjust their approach because they are conscious of the range of verbal and nonverbal responses, and constantly check that they are being understood.

As with all skills, the route to expertise is practice. **Habit 2** involves training your senses by noticing more about the environment in which you live and work. You can do this in a general way by imagining yourself as a stranger seeing the environment for the first time. You may be surprised at what you see – like the thimble, things that have been there all the time but which you've never noticed before. You'll be surprised at what you can hear when you pause to become aware of the different sounds you can hear at any one time. You'll begin to notice how powerfully smells can evoke forgotten memories (the olfactory nerves in the nasal cavity are close to the part of the brain which deals with memory and emotions).

Habit 2 is also about paying close attention to the people with whom you come into contact. Without resorting to staring (which could get you into trouble) you can either decide to notice a particular feature of everyone you come into contact with for a day, or you can see how much you can notice that you weren't aware of previously (see Figure 5). Once you've noticed the subtle features of

	NOTICE:
Voice	tone/pitch/pace/inflection/accent
Skin	colour/shininess/muscle-tone
Eyes	Movements: up/down/left/right/ combinations
	dilation of pupils/widening/degree of Eye-contact
Facial expressions	Eyebrow movements, smiles, frowns, grimaces, muscle-twitching
Lip size	thinning
Head	angled to one side/held up/down
Body posture	bent/upright
Gestures	movement of legs/arms/hand gestures/ foot-tapping/fidgeting

Figure 5   Sensory acuity: some things to look out for

other people's physiology and demeanour, you can begin to notice more and more how people change from minute to minute. This is vital preparation for **Habit 5**.

The meaning of your behaviour is the response you get[10]

As with all things in which we develop skill, at first we are consciously aware of what we are doing, but after a great deal of practice we develop unconscious performance. As with riding a bike, or with touch-typing. I learned to touch-type many years ago, and consider myself pretty speedy on a keyboard. But if you asked me to tell you the order of the letters on the keyboard, I would struggle to do so. I would need to use my fingers to type out a word in order mentally to recollect the order of the keys. Constant practice at typing has led to a development of neural networking that allows for very rapid processing and action.[11] So that it now appears I can touch-type without referring to any mental memory of the order of the keys.

Can we relate this example to professional expertise such as teaching? Professional expertise is much more complicated than touch-typing, and will take several years to acquire. Yet we have the same neurology to develop both, and if we continue with the example of touch-typing we can understand more of how it works. I will 'know' if I've typed a wrong letter − my sense of feel will tell me if I've made a mistake. My sense of feel has been developed with experience, by taking note of feedback in the form of the physical sensation when my fingers strike the right key, and the accuracy of the finished product. In developing teaching professionalism, feedback will come from the reactions of pupils, comments from colleagues and from your own reflection and self-evaluation. Both extended practice and feedback are necessary to achieve professional competence.[12] Good teachers know that feedback is an essential element in developing self-knowledge and behavioural flexibility.

The most obvious way we gain feedback on our behaviour is from the response of other people. If people respond positively towards us, we can know that our behaviour is fit for purpose. Equally, if we encounter resistance, then we will know that we need to consider how our own behaviour may be triggering a resistance.

There are two ways we can do this. We can reflect on our behaviour, think about what it might be about our behaviour that could cause resistance or contribute to an unsatisfactory outcome, and consider alternative strategies (see **Habits 5** and **7**). Or we could try a direct approach. That is, when we find ourselves working with people where the relationship is unsatisfactory, we could ask the other people how we might change our behaviour to improve the relationship.

If your first reaction to that statement is something along the lines of 'What if it's just that the other people are being really difficult?' look back at the subheading of this section. It suggests that we may have a certain intention, but if other people perceive our behaviour differently, then our intention is lost. So if we want to find out how we can achieve our intention, we need to find out how we are coming across to other people. The knowledge we gain from this will help us adjust our behaviour to achieve a more productive outcome. Here comes the 'F' word again – flexibility. Flexibility develops from being prepared to accept that we can't always assume our intention is perceived accurately by other people. We can judge whether it is by the reaction, or we can ask other people for their assessment of our behaviour. As with touch-typing, the only way we will know if we've struck the right key is by the feedback we get: either from the outcome we achieve or by what people tell us.

The Johari Window (Figure 6) shows how this can help us to discover more about ourselves. It shows there is information that we know about ourselves, some of which we reveal to other people. We can never know exactly how other people perceive us – that is the 'Blind' area. There are things about ourselves that we are hesitant about revealing – that is the 'Hidden' area. **Habit 2** involves being more open about ourselves and asking others for feedback. **Habit 2** is seeking to extend the 'Open' window, which improves relationships.

The *way* in which we ask for feedback from other people of course has a fundamental relationship to the value of the feedback we receive. We may test the quality of a relationship by blithely asking, 'How was it for you?', but the chances are we would not get a response that would be of much value to our learning and development. Responses such as 'fine', 'OK with me' or 'just great' may give us a nice warm feeling about ourselves, but they don't really give us anything to work with to develop professionally.

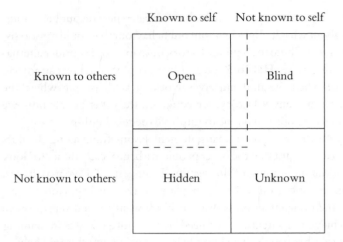

Figure 6   The Johari Window
Source: Luft 1969.

Professional empowerment can only come from feedback that specifically describes our behaviour, and relates to those behaviours under our control. For instance, it's not much use to us for someone to tell us our accent gets on their nerves, but it is useful to be told that we would sound more convincing if we used a different tone of voice. It could be discouraging to be told that our appearance can be offputting, but it's helpful to be told that if we stood in a different way, or gesticulated less when talking, then we would carry more of an air of authority. It's not particularly helpful to be told we shouldn't slouch, but it's valuable feedback to know that we could improve relationships if we used more eye-contact when talking to other people.

Habit 2 means having the confidence to ask for the feedback we need to grow professionally. If the feedback we receive doesn't meet with the checklist criteria (see Pause for Thought 6) we can use open questions to draw out more helpful information, for example:

- How exactly did my behaviour exacerbate the situation?
- What specifically was it about what I said that wasn't helpful?
- What else could I have done?
- What else could I have said?
- I felt uncomfortable in that situation, what could I have done about it?
- How could I have been more assertive?

- Did I come across as bossy? What can I do about that?
- Did I sound disrespectful? How could I have said things differently?

And of course we should not forget the value of positive feedback:

- I felt I handled that situation very well. What do you think?
- I feel I gained in confidence by dealing with that. Did I seem more confident?
- I thought I kept my voice calm and controlled. How did it sound to you?

Pause for Thought 6: Feedback – nourishment or punishment[13]

Nourishment	Punishment
Deals with behaviour, not the person	Deals with the person, not the behaviour
Describes the behaviour	Makes a judgement on behaviour
Is specific and direct	Is general and woolly
Focuses on behaviours the receiver can control	Refers to behaviours outside the receiver's control
Receiver's needs are the focus	Is distorted by sender's needs
Includes real feelings	Feelings are concealed, denied, misrepresented or distorted
Affirms the receiver's worth	Inflates the sender's worth

Remember: there's no failure, only feedback.[14]

A foundation for flexibility

Habit 2 encourages mental and behavioural flexibility. But making flexibility a single goal will not ensure professional empowerment. Taken to its extreme, flexibility of thought and action could result in being seduced into the idea that change and innovation are the only goals worth pursuing. The sociologist Richard Sennett has pointed out the implications of today's society searching for ways to destroy the evils of routine by creating more flexible institutions; his concern is that the practices of flexibility focus mostly on the forces bending people.[15]

Sennett claims that in advocating flexibility, those who are in control of organizations assume flexibility involves change, when in fact it is change of a particular sort. It is not the sort of change that maintains links with what went before, rather there is rupture because the change seeks to reinvent institutions decisively and irrevocably. Teachers of longstanding will have experienced changing political whims that have insisted change is in the interests of developing a more flexible educational system. But these changes have frequently been enforced on the basis of a political agenda rather than with consultation or consideration of the potential effects on educational experience.

The basis of my call for flexibility is rather different. While Sennett is describing the pressure for flexibility urged upon organizations, what I am advocating is individual mental and behavioural flexibility to empower us to cope with an increasingly complex working environment. A rigid stance of 'This is the way we've always done it' can no longer be justified. We have to be open and knowledgeable about our own profession so that we can adapt to changes where they can be beneficial. And from an informed base we also need to be prepared to challenge where change is for the sake of change. However, the warnings from Sennett's writings alert us to an essential element to be included if flexibility is to be successful. There's a clue in the original meaning of the word 'flexibility' – which was derived from the observation that, although a tree may bend in the wind, its branches spring back to their original position.[16]

So an essential element in being able to exhibit flexible behaviour is something that will ensure that we 'spring back' to some sort of grounded position. **Habit 1** describes one way: we can practise a range of behaviours in different roles, if we have a clear sense of identity to ground us. And there's another practical way to ensure that we can spring back emotionally to where we want to be – we can make use of the process of 'anchoring'.

Anchors

Part of empowerment is accepting that we can be in control of our whole selves, not just managers of our behaviour. To be in control of ourselves we need to accept that we can manage our 'state' whenever we need to. By 'state' I mean that combination of mental, physical and emotional conditions that we experience at any one time. (There will be more on this in **Habits 3** and **6**).

Just think for a moment of the naturally occurring external factors that influence your 'state'. Are there pieces of music that put you into a particular mood in an instant? My son and daughter always played lively music to get them into the mood for an evening out – and very loudly! On the other hand there may be a piece of music you find particularly calming. And have you ever used music to establish a particular mood with your class? I used this to great effect when I was teaching – young people who had never even heard of Mozart or Vivaldi came to welcome their accompaniment to classwork.

And what about pictorial images? Do you have photographs of loved ones that you carry with you because every time you look at them you get a particular warm feeling? Are there holiday photographs that give you an instant replay of the happy times you enjoyed? Have you chosen posters or displays because you want to cultivate a particular emotional climate in your classroom?

Yet again are there certain objects that have the feel of a comfort-blanket to you? I have two pebbles of crystal that were given to me by a student some years ago. They remind me of the love and respect with which they were given. Every so often I take them out and roll them between my fingers. There's something very soothing yet stimulating about the feel of the stones.

There's nothing spectacularly new about all this. Pavlov established the principle with his experiments with dogs in the early years of the last century. He showed that if you associated an external signal (a bell) with the provision of food, eventually the animal would salivate at the sound of the bell even when the food didn't arrive. In just the same way, something we see, hear or touch (or smell or taste) can trigger an emotional or physiological response.

The examples above have all illustrated how an external trigger can initiate a particular positive 'state'. And of course the principle works in reverse. Some of the first work in the 1920s in applying Pavlov's findings to humans established fear in an infant by association.[17] For me, the sound of a dentist's drill will make my mouth water, I cringe at the feel of fish scales, and there are plenty of visual images I can't look at because they make me feel sick. I imagine it won't be too difficult to think of examples for yourself.

But why would we want to do that? Why would we want to continue responding to external stimuli in a negative way? Why not apply the principle for our own benefit? Knowing that there are times when we will need to 'spring back' to a certain grounded emotional and physiological state, why not use an external trigger to enable us to do this?

Anchors allow us to do just that. The term 'anchor' is aptly chosen for our purposes if you think about the function of an anchor. An anchor secures a ship in a steady position. An anchor is strong and weighty enough to withstand the buffeting of wind and weather. An anchor is carried with the ship and put to use when needed.

You will already have objects or opportunities in your life that give you a 'feel good' factor. After reading this, you may be able to think of more you can set up for yourself, because the more the better. And we can empower ourselves further by setting up anchors that will stabilize us in a particular positive state (see Pause for Thought 7). Highly effective teachers can respond to situations, exhibit a range of flexible behaviours, yet not be blown off course by the demands being made on them. They can access their inner resources when they need to stabilize themselves into a congruent mental, emotional and physical state.

Pause for Thought 7: Setting a kinaesthetic anchor

This anchor will be in the form of a touch. This is useful because it does not depend upon any external factor – you can trigger the anchor any time, any place, anywhere.

First decide how you are going to set your anchor. It could be by touching a particular knuckle, by placing two fingers together, by touching a particular spot on a wrist or arm. Be quite specific about this, because you will need to use exactly the same spot every time you want to trigger the anchor. Now start the process:

1 Remember a time when you experienced a feeling of being in complete control of yourself. A time when you felt confident, when your mental, physical and emotional powers felt in alignment.

2 As you remember the time, immerse yourself into the memory. See again what was happening, hear the sounds, re-experience the feeling of confidence, of being in total control.

3 As you reach the point of fully experiencing the feeling, touch the spot you have decided upon for a few seconds.

4 Step back out of the memory. Look around you and notice something particular in your surroundings. Break the mental and emotional state completely.

5 Repeat the process from Step 2 twice more, using the same memory and the same anchor spot. Remember to 'break state' cleanly each time.

6 Now test the anchor by touching the spot. If you have set the anchor successfully, you will be able to experience the feeling without having to access the original memory.

Well done! You now have that feeling at your command. You can get back to that confident, in-control feeling whenever you need to.

Conclusion

The complexity of a teacher's working life means you will have to make a thousand decisions in any one day: how to respond to an individual pupil, how to speak to a parent, how to advise a colleague, how to adapt a planned lesson to accommodate different learning styles. We have choice in everything, and our approach will depend upon choices that we make. We can choose to immerse ourselves in busy work which becomes routinized action. Or we can adopt **Habit 2** and open our senses to the opportunities presented to develop flexibility in thinking and behaviour. Even some of the most important scientific discoveries came about because someone paid more attention to a humdrum event than the situation appeared to warrant. Such as Archimedes, lowering himself into the bath. If he had merely thought 'Darn it, I've got the floor wet again, what will the missus say?', we would have had to wait another few hundred years to understand the principle of fluid displacement.[18]

Habit 2 involves being alert to the information from our senses to develop the ability to act flexibly and intuitively. It means being aware and responsive to differences in students and colleagues. It means actively identifying the sort of feedback that will enable us to develop a flexible range of behaviours. Good teachers recognize the need to adjust their own behaviour if students are not learning, or if they are not getting the response from others that they are seeking.

Teaching is a demanding profession, but you can develop the resources to withstand the buffeting of its demands. Empowerment comes from being in control of your whole self, not just from managing your behaviour. You can adapt to change where it is beneficial, but be prepared to challenge it when it is not, or when it is just change for its own sake. **Habit 2** means being able to access your inner resources to act effectively in what is an increasingly complex working environment.

Reflection: The learning pathway to empowered professionalism

At first – when we don't know what we don't know – we are in a state of *unconscious incompetence*.

As we become aware of the learning we need to accomplish, we move to *conscious incompetence*.

Once we know what we need to do, we still need conscious awareness to put into practice the new skills or knowledge. We are now at a stage of *conscious competence*.

When we become experienced we are able to act and respond to situations without conscious thought, apparently intuitively. We are at the stage of *unconscious competence*.*

---

* Empowerment health warning!
We can get stuck here so that we think we know all we need to know to function as a professional. Empowerment means taking the time and effort *consciously* to check out how we are doing, reflecting on the feedback we are getting from our senses and from other people, and adjusting our behaviour accordingly. If we don't constantly adjust and monitor our map of the world, it will soon become out of date.

Notes

1. One of the presuppositions of neuro-linguistic programming.
2. Ehrenberg 1991.
3. Birgerstam 2002.
4. Atkinson and Claxton 2000: 7.
5. Atkinson 2000: 53–65.
6. Dennett 1991: 337.
7. Eraut 2000: 255–68.
8. Brown and Coles 2000: 165–81.
9. Brande 1934.
10. Another of the presuppositions of neurolinguistic programming. If there are no failures in behaviour or communication, only responses and feedback, it therefore follows that if you are not getting the response you want, you should do something different. (See Appendix 1.)
11. Greenfield 1997.
12. Atkinson 2000: 69–83.
13. See Stenhouse Consulting.
14. Another of the principles of neuro-linguistic programming. See Appendix 1.
15. Sennett 1998: 46.
16. Ibid.
17. The Case of Little Albert. See Watson and Rayner 1920.
18. Csikszentmihalyi 1997: 104.

Habit 3: Taking action on stress

When work is a pleasure, life is a joy! When work is a duty, life is slavery.[1]

Notions of 'stress' are now so commonplace that it is easy to forget that stress is a comparatively recent phenomenon in relation to the human condition. 'Stress' is still used to indicate forces applied to a body (as in engineering), or the emphasis placed on a word, but we have also come to accept 'stress' as a word that refers to the physical, emotional or mental strain on human beings. Certainly in the Western world we are better fed and housed, and have a longer life-expectancy than our ancestors in previous centuries. But the conditions of the twentieth century that have brought improvements in our general health and well-being have also given rise to detrimental physical and mental effects as a result of the way we organize our life and work.

The incidence and interest in workplace stress grew alongside the growth of organizations and the increasing complexity of our modern world. As organizations became larger and more complex, and as life began to be lived at a faster pace, it also became increasingly evident that modern lifestyles were exacting a price in respect of stress-related illness. The annual National Stress Awareness Day in the UK is an indicator that stress is now an acknowledged part of our way of life.

Researchers became interested in this phenomenon. They prioritized lists of potential stress-inducing life events, so that you could work out whether you had sufficient high-scoring events in your lifestyle to place you in danger of suffering the effects of stress. The most stress-inducing jobs were prioritized (teaching always came very high amongst those). And psychologists attempted to define why some people succumbed to the physical and mental effects of stress and others didn't. Was it because of some particular characteristics of personality, or did some people develop better skills at dealing with stress than others?

In teaching we cannot avoid the significance of the work context as an influencing factor in stress: 40 per cent of the teaching profession report high levels of stress, which is far greater than both nurses and managers in all other public sectors. If we accept that it is highly unlikely that the teaching profession attracts a majority of those people with the least resilience to stress, then we must conclude that it is something about conditions of work that result in this high incidence.

Highly effective teachers understand how stress can cause deterioration in mental and physical health, and they are able to tackle and deal with their own conditions of work that are stress-inducing. **Habit 3** means they are able to draw on a range of strategies to maintain their mental health and physical energy. Highly effective teachers have also recognized and developed the other two key habits that are of crucial importance in taking action against stress.

The first of these is **Habit 4: Taking your time**. Highly effective teachers understand their approach to our most valuable resource – time – and develop the skills to prioritize and achieve a work–life balance. They know that seeking to improve time-management skills does not just mean enabling ourselves to do more in the time available – although that can obviously be an outcome. Improving time-management can also equip us to recognize whether what we are trying to do really is unmanageable and likely to impact negatively on our ability to achieve work–life balance. Achieving more at work is also about recognizing when our body needs rest and relaxation, or exercise and physical stimulation. Adopting **Habit 4** enables us to build into our lifestyle opportunities to conserve and energize our physical and mental resources.

Highly effective teachers have also adopted **Habit 7: Practising the behaviours of influence**. While a great deal of stress can be generated by the feeling of being overwhelmed by work, the role other people play in relation to our workload can also be a source of stress. Being able to deal assertively with other people is a crucial stress-avoidance skill. Highly effective teachers have learned two factors about assertive behaviour. Firstly, they understand and accept that we all have certain rights of equality as human beings. Secondly, they have developed skills to be able to deal with relationships that threaten their self-esteem and impact upon their ability to achieve a work–life balance.

Both **Habit 4** and **Habit 6** are about achieving personal control. Together with **Habit 2** they empower us to take control in order to achieve a good work–life balance, and take action against stress. For it is when we feel 'out of control' that we are likely to succumb to the debilitating effects of feeling stressed.

The effects of stress

Part of taking control means understanding the stress our modern life can inflict on bodies designed for the activities of a much earlier age. We may have evolved 'new' brains, we may live in a highly technological age, but our bodies still retain the functional requirements of life thousands of years ago. As human beings we are exquisitely adapted to recognize and respond to threats to survival that come in the form of sudden dramatic events. If someone claps their hands we will jump, calling forth a genetically encoded memory of sabre-toothed tigers springing from the bush.[2] We may not come across sabre-toothed tigers too often in our modern lives, but our nervous systems still retain a 'startle' response. Our systems are designed to protect us by responding when our brains signal 'Danger!' without knowing what form that danger is taking. In our modern lifestyle it could be the prospect of an interview, facing a rebellious class or dealing with an angry parent, rather than anything literally life-threatening.

When this happens, our involuntary nervous system kicks in. Hormones are released and signals sent to various parts of our bodies. Our muscles tense, preparing for a 'fight-or-flight' response. Our bloodstream diverts energy from our digestive system to enable the muscles to prepare for a response. Breathing-rate speeds up. Sweating increases to help cool the body. Saliva dries up, leaving us with a dry mouth. Heart rate speeds up and blood pressure rises. The liver releases sugar to provide quick energy. Immune responses decrease: useful in the short term to allow for a massive response to an immediate threat, but harmful over a long period as it reduces our ability to resist infection.[3]

In a less extreme form these responses may happen many times each day. If an immediate physical response is needed – such as if you have to take quick physical action to ensure the safety of a child – the body will soon recover from the initial adrenalin surge. But it's the constant arousal of fight-or-flight responses that means the body will often get tense – ready for action, but no action is taken. Indeed, some people reach a point where they hardly notice what's happening. And tension without action leads to chronic stress.[4]

In the short term the accumulated tension can result in physical aches and pains, headaches, stomach-upsets or rashes. Long term, if unresolved, the tension can lead to more serious signs of disease. Maintaining the body in a constant state of arousal can upset the normal control of blood pressure, lead to complaints such as stomach ulcers and seriously affect the body's ability to maintain a healthy immune system for fighting disease. And resorting to short-term fixes, such as smoking, drinking too much alcohol or overeating, can also damage health in the long-run.

There is also the emotional element that results from stress. Without any language to describe them, our ancestors experienced emotions as brain-states and bodily responses.[5] The emotional reaction is a very rapid-response mechanism – it happens in milliseconds. It is this speed of reaction that would have ensured the survival of our ancestors. (Our ancestors were more instinctively and less linguistically orientated than ourselves, but as with the 'startle' response, certain emotional processing functions are preserved within the human brain.)[6]

The exact relationship between our thinking and our emotions is an issue that has engaged psychologists for most of the twentieth century. For our purposes, it is sufficient that we recognize the crucial difference between ourselves and our ancestors; the difference that has ensured our survival as the cleverest creatures on the planet. That difference is of course that our brains have evolved two important functions: the ability to think and reason, and to use language. We can be *consciously* aware that we are feeling an emotion, and we have language to be able to put a name to that emotion and differentiate between fear, anxiety, terror, apprehension and the like.[7]

Being more aware of our emotions doesn't mean we can always control their physical effects on us. The link between emotional distress and the suppression of the immune system is now well known.[8] But while our modern lives may have more potential for stress, we have extra equipment – reasoning and language – to be able to deal with it. We can work out our approach to time and how it impacts upon our stress levels (**Habit 4**). We can change the language we use to improve working relationships with others (**Habit 6**). And in taking action on stress we can develop strategies at all levels – physical, mental and emotional – to empower ourselves to achieve a good work–life balance. Highly effective teachers take action to keep themselves permanently off the cycle of stressful event–automatic response that leads to tension and stress-related illness.

Empowerment points	Taking action
The event that causes stress	Change the situation
The way you 'see' the event	Change the thoughts
The way you feel about the event	Change the feelings
Your physical response	Release the tension
Taking action	Doing things differently to get yourself off the stressor–response cycle

Figure 7   Taking action on stress
Source: Open University 1992.

Change the situation

It can sometimes be quite hard to identify the exact cause of stress. Like the old adage of someone having a bad day at the office, then coming home and kicking the cat, we can react emotionally against someone or something that has nothing to do with the 'stressor'. We may know that we feel stressed, but it can take careful thought to identify the source.

This is where neuro-logical levels (Figure 2) can be a useful aid. Thinking through the levels can help pin down the exact source of stress.

For instance, is there something about your *environment* that can be changed to make you feel and act differently? Taking the time to de-clutter your desk or rearrange your classroom could be something that could make your work a lot easier. Are you putting an unnatural strain on your body by the way you drive a car, or the way you sit at a computer? Are you creating physical tension by staying in one posture for too long without a break or without releasing the tension by taking exercise?

Or is there something about your *behaviour* that can be changed to achieve more equitable relationships with other people? (See **Habit 7**.) If there is an issue with a certain pupil or colleague that is a source of stress, have you thought about how you could change your behaviour towards them? How could you behave differently to improve the relationship?

On reflection, you may think that there is some strain on your *capability* to undertake the work you are being asked to do, and that you would benefit from further study or specific training. Feedback and advice from a colleague might be helpful here, and researching what resources you could access to improve your capability.

And in an area that will need considerable thought, you may come to a conclusion that the mismatch between your own *beliefs and values* and those of the organization you work for is a major source of stress. A realization such as this can lead to very big changes indeed.

Change the thoughts 1: recognizing choices

It may often seem that we have no control over events: that stressful situations are outside our control. But for most of us there's an element of choice in most things – the real issue is whether we can recognize and are prepared to exercise it.

I remember David, who was a highly effective classroom teacher. He also had the aptitude and leadership qualities of an excellent head-teacher had he chosen to pursue his career in that direction. But David had recognized that for him job-satisfaction came from the interaction with his students, from the knowledge that he was contributing to the development of young minds, that he could exert a positive influence upon the self-esteem and confidence of his students. David had realized that, for him, this was where the real value of his professional role lay, and he had made a positive choice not to pursue progression to a managerial position.

On the other hand, Gaynor was a headteacher for whom promotion to that role had brought a great deal of unhappiness. She too had been a good teacher, yet she struggled to cope with the very different requirements of the management and leadership role in a primary school. Perhaps a management role had come too soon for her; perhaps she needed to build her confidence; perhaps she needed to develop the skills of leading adults as well as children. Whatever the reason, the fault lay in not thinking about what she really wanted from her professional life, or where her strengths lay. Rather, she had sought promotion simply believing it was the thing to do. Having achieved it, she gained little satisfaction from the day-to-day challenges. Instead, she routinely moaned about not being able to motivate her staff, complained about how much work she had to do because she couldn't depend upon anyone, and regaled the rest of the staff with details of the difficult parents she had to deal with. Not surprisingly, this approach led eventually to long-term sick-leave due to stress-related illness.

Thankfully, our profession has now moved to recognize excellence in teaching so that a teacher who chooses to stay in the classroom can gain the appropriate financial reward. But the point about choice is that we don't always think carefully enough about what is the right choice for us, or even recognize that we have choices in most things. Unless we think through the right choice for ourselves, we can be led to believe that what other people do is what we ourselves must do. In this connection, changing the thoughts can mean thinking outside the box to identify the right choice for ourselves, rather than accepting other people's thoughts on what 'should' be the right choice for us.

Pause for Thought 8: What motivates you?

The panel were interviewing for a management post in a comprehensive school. All the candidates were well-qualified and experienced, and it was difficult to choose between them. All candidates had been asked the same questions, so the panel decided to review each candidate's response to the questions in turn. The first question had been: 'Why are you applying for this post?'
Gareth's response had been:

Well I feel it's something I should be looking to do now, I mean move to a management responsibility. I don't want to reach retirement age and still be a classroom teacher. And I think I could manage the extra responsibilities. If I'm given a deadline I always meet it because I don't like to think about the consequences if I don't. I'm always careful in starting something new, so I'd make sure I knew everything about the new responsibilities so I didn't make a mistake. And one thing I know I'd be good at would be pointing out to other staff the potential hazards if there were any suggestions for new ways of working.

Lucy's response had been:

My long-term aim is to progress to a headteacher post. I think this post would be the first step towards that. I haven't had any management responsibility yet, but I think I could do this job. I think it would be quite a challenge and I like challenges. I'm quite motivated by the thought of the extra responsibilities, such as having to manage other staff. I think it would stretch me, and that's what I need; I need something to work towards.

What motivates *you*? Are you like Gareth, motivated to move away from what you want to avoid, rather than towards what you want to achieve? Are you motivated to meet deadlines in order to avoid any negative consequences? Do you always think about what could go wrong, so have trouble thinking about what you really want to achieve? Or are you more like Lucy, motivated by a carrot rather than a stick? Are you motivated by a desire for things you want to have or goals you want to achieve? Does this sometimes mean you plunge into new ventures without thinking through the possible negative consequences? Do you think Gareth and Lucy might create stress for themselves in some circumstances due to their thinking? How could they adjust their thinking to reduce the potential for stress?

Change the thoughts 2: 'change the lights'

Shakespeare understood a lot about human nature. One of his characters says about thinking that there's nothing either good or bad, but thinking makes it so.[9] Indeed we have a choice in how we think about things, as with everything else. Gaynor viewed the cause of the difficulties she encountered mainly as the non-cooperation of the people with whom she came into contact. As long as she chose to think this way, she continued to carry a sense of grievance about the situation she was in; to harbour negative thoughts that eventually were to become too heavy to bear and which led to illness. She didn't just see her glass as half-empty, she thought someone else had drunk the lot!

How could Gaynor have thought differently? She could have thought of her difficulties as *challenges*: challenges that would spur her on to acquire a wider range of experience. She could have viewed relationships with staff and parents as *opportunities* for her to develop wider skill-base to enable her to deal successfully with different people. Instead of thinking of herself as failing, she could have thought of her experiences as *feedback* that would enable her to develop and grow as an empowered professional.[10] Not only could her glass have been half-full, it could have been positively overflowing!

'Change the lights', is a metaphor that helps me remember there are always alternatives: there is always a different way of thinking about a situation. It's taken from what happens in the theatre, from the different effects that can be achieved with stage-lighting. Take pantomimes for instance. You may remember that they frequently open with a brightly lit scene, usually a village square, where colourfully dressed villagers gather and the main characters are introduced. In contrast, further on in the production will be a scene where the hero faces danger and the battle between Good and Evil ensues. Whether this takes place in a dark cave or somewhere deep in a forest the aim is to create an effect that elicits 'oohs' and 'aahs' from an audience of small children. The previously bright lights are dimmed and shades of green or red are introduced with eerie effect. A change of scenery alone would not create a different atmosphere. But change the lights, and the effect is totally different: it's the same stage and the same cast as in the cheerful village scene, but the production team have been able to create different feelings in the audience by a change of lighting.

You can use the same strategy for yourself to change negative feelings into feelings that are more likely to empower you. Using 'change the lights' as a trigger, you can change the thoughts to change the meaning you are attaching to a situation, which will then change the way you feel about it. It will need you to be proactive in deliberately throwing the switch and changing the thoughts. But the effects can be dramatic.

A good way to start is to use some questions to challenge the way you are *re*-presenting a situation. Here are some examples (as you practise you'll be able to add more of your own):

- What's the learning in this for me?
- What's the opportunity in this for me?
- How can I use this experience to improve my teaching?
- What would [someone you admire] do in this situation?
- Where's the humour in this?
- How can I turn what appears to be a threat into an opportunity?
- How does this situation help me to develop and grow as an *empowered professional*?

Change the feelings: 'writing it out'

Sometimes it can seem that negative thoughts and feelings linger despite your efforts to 'change the lights'. When this happens, unless you take action on them, negative emotions can fester inside. A small event can easily attain the properties of a personal insult if you choose to dwell on it that way. Then it becomes like steam in a kettle and will find an outlet to force its way out. Negative feelings can find an outlet in an 'over-the-top' reaction towards another person, even someone unconnected with the original perceived insult.

You may also find it difficult to 'change the lights' in a situation that has caused you worry or concern. Worry and anxiety can cause lack of sleep and distract you from performing at your best at work. If you allow it to, worry can also grow to monstrous proportions unrelated to the original extent of the cause and can threaten your overall health and well-being.

So if negative thoughts and feelings persist, or if worry and anxiety are in danger of getting out of hand, you need a way to take action to deal with them. An action that is quick, easy and effective; an action that will empower you to leave the negativity or worry aside so that you can get on with teaching. This is where 'writing it out' of your system can help. There is choice in this as in everything else: different forms suit different situations.

Writing it out 1

I have great admiration for a colleague who confessed that she kept a journal, and that she wrote in it daily. I've tried it myself, although I've never succeeded in maintaining it on a daily basis. However, having established the practice, I find that I often turn to my journal when I want to record an event, and more importantly, to express how I feel about it. There's something about the privacy of a journal, of writing something that no one else will see, that allows you to express yourself honestly. The point is that, in order to *write out* your emotions or worries, you have to think about them. And it's just this process that allows you to come to understand your feelings and come to terms with them. It's as if your journal were your very own therapist, and *writing it out* your 'talking cure'.

Writing it out 2

Unresolved emotion and worry can prove a hindrance to a good night's sleep. If you don't want the formality of a journal, you can still gain the same effect by keeping a notebook and pen at the side of the bed. If sleep evades you when negative thoughts persist, just switch on the bedside light and *write them out*. Your writing could be just jottings, it doesn't have to be in any presentable form because, again, no one will see it. But, having released the thoughts into the notebook, you will find you've cleared your mind to enable you to sleep.

Writing it out 3

You may find this method is best if you have unresolved emotions following an argument or confrontation with another person. You may not have taken the opportunity to deal with the other person assertively (see **Habit 7**), and you may be agonizing over this as a lost opportunity. You could then gain closure for yourself by *writing it out* in a letter to the other person expressing exactly how you feel. You may decide not to send the letter – although there may be situations where you might wish to do so. It's real use is as a therapeutic tool for you to deal with residual negative emotions.

It's important to take a disciplined approach to this particular strategy. Compose the letter with care because you want the recipient to take notice of it. Rather than starting by pouring out your feelings, as in the first two 'writing it out', examples, this strategy necessitates examining possible exaggerations or assumptions on your part. As with any other letter-writing, adopt a businesslike, factual approach that aims to make the other person appreciate your point of view:

- Describe the unsatisfactory event.
- Identify the feelings you experienced at the time.

- Check that in rethinking you're not exaggerating the facts *or* the feelings.
- Challenge any faulty self-talk that's making assumptions or exaggerating the facts or feelings.
- Describe the feelings in realistic terms. Did you feel concerned, annoyed, disappointed, belittled, embarrassed, sad, angry?
- Write out a description of the facts of the event, and your feelings, making sure that you are realistic and objective, resist inflammatory language and use 'I' statements (e.g., 'I felt very embarrassed by this situation').

Use the last paragraph of the letter to draw conclusions. Do you want to negotiate a different relationship between yourself and the other person? Has something happened that you feel is very unfair and you would like to be rectified? Can you offer to act in a different way yourself to improve the situation between you and the other person?

Sign the letter and put it away somewhere safe overnight. Take it out and reread it another day and decide whether you want to send it or not.

Creating distance to avoid negative stress

Even when you've been diligent in using these strategies to avoid the build-up of harmful stress, there may still be some issues that you find yourself unable to deal with. The persistence of unresolved negative feelings or worry can then be a mental distraction and will sap your physical energy. Negative emotions in particular produce 'psychic entrophy' in the mind – a state in which we cannot attend effectively to tasks, because we need to restore our inner subjective order.[11]

There can be many reasons why you may be unable to resolve an issue. An emotion or feeling of being ill-used may be so strong that it defies all your efforts to eliminate it. You may not yet have reached a level of understanding where you know what to do about a stressful situation. You have yet to develop the skills to deal with an issue. It may be that there is nothing you *can* do about a situation, but you still worry about it.

In cases like these, you need a strategy that will distance you from the worry or negative feelings to protect you from their debilitating effects. It's not good for your psychological health simply to bury a

Settle yourself somewhere quiet where you are not likely to be disturbed. Make sure you are physically as relaxed as you can be. Say to yourself that you are going to concentrate wholly on this process, and not let any other thoughts distract you.

Now with your mind's eye you can see a basket in front of you. It's square and quite large and very sturdy. You can see the wicker plaited in and out and you know how strong it is. Reach out with your hands and measure the square shape and feel the strength of the wicker.

Now think about the worry or negative feelings you want to deal with. Use your hands to gather up all the feelings in front of you. Make absolutely sure that you have all the feelings you want to deal with gathered mentally in your hands. If something has escaped, pull it back in. If you think you're ignoring something, be honest and include it.

When you're quite certain you have all the feelings, dump them in the basket.

Now you notice that this basket has some other features. Looking upwards you can see that suspended over it is a very large balloon. Run your eyes over the colours and patterns. You can sense that the balloon is straining to lift the basket.

Now that you look downwards, you can see that the basket is secured by a strong rope. The thickness of the coils is holding the basket in place. You can hear the sounds of stress on the rope as the balloon is straining to be freed.

Reach down and release the rope from where it is secured. Now slowly and carefully, hand over hand, play out the rope so that the balloon takes the basket up and away.

Keep your mind's eye on the balloon as it takes the basket away from you, as it gets smaller and smaller, away into the distance. With your eye you can follow the rope, still attached to the basket.

Take a deep breath and close your eyes. You have the image of the balloon and the basket and the rope linking you to them recorded in your mind's eye. You know that if you choose, you can pull on the rope and bring back the basket and deal with the negative feelings and worries. You may decide to do that one day. One day you will be stronger and able to deal with them. For the moment they are secure and out of harm's way.

Open your eyes and get on with your life.

Figure 8   Balloon and the basket

negative emotion, but you *can* deal with it in such a way that you put it 'on hold' until such time that you are more able to come to terms with it. There may not be anything you can do at the present time to resolve a situation that you're worrying about, but by keeping it 'on hold' – keeping it at a safe distance – you can return to it at a time when you have developed a better understanding to be able to deal with it. In the meantime, you will save the drain on your energy and avoid possible sleepless nights.

Figure 8 gives an example of how you can do this. I've used this metaphor for many years and found it to be effective. It was also gratifying to talk to an former teaching colleague recently and find that she was continuing to use it, some ten years after I first introduced it to her. Not only that, but she was also passing it on to pupils as a way of dealing with their worry about exams.

While this works for me, it's also useful to be able to devise your own metaphor, something that is meaningful for you. Another colleague had dealt with the feelings from a particularly upsetting relationship by using the metaphor of a boat. She could see it in her mind's eye very clearly: it was brightly painted with a colourful sail, and it bobbed away down a river taking the negative effects of the emotion with it. Whatever you find works for you, use it. Just keep to the principle that although you may not be able to resolve the worry or negative feelings at the moment, they are being taken care of for the time being to allow you to get on with your life.

Finding 'flow'

Habit 3 has been about dealing with the negative effects of stress, when the level of stress becomes such that there is a need to take action to deal with it. On the other hand, highly effective teachers have discovered that the *right level* of stress can energize and excite them. Professor Mihalyi Csikszentmihalyi has spent his life researching people involved in challenging activities – from rock-climbing, dancing and chess to leading teams, performing surgery and composing music.[12] For many people, it is the challenge that takes this work from being a chore to an adventure. For these people, the right level of stress is a source of excitement and motivation.

It's that 'right level of stress' that makes the difference between being completely absorbed and energized by your work, or finding it an anxiety-inducing occupation. Csikszentmihalyi describes the quality of an experience as 'flow' – the experience of complete immersion in an activity, maintaining intense concentration on what we are doing, yet at the same time being aware of everything around us. It is a time of effortless action when our consciousness is full of experiences, and these experiences are in harmony with each other.[13]

The quality of the experience of 'flow' comes from the relationship between the challenge and the skills to be able to meet the challenge. 'Flow' tends to occur when a person's skills are fully involved in overcoming a challenge that is just about manageable. If the challenges are too great, we can get frustrated, then worried, and eventually anxious. If the challenges are too low in relation to the level of skill, this can lead to boredom. If both challenges and skills are low, this can lead to apathy. It's when challenges are matched with skills that the deep involvement that sets 'flow' apart from the experience of ordinary life is likely to occur.[14]

Csikszentmihalyi is not suggesting that we can all achieve 'flow' all the time in our daily lives. A typical day will include spells of anxiety or boredom. 'Flow' experiences provide flashes of intense living against the routine of our daily lives.[15] But the idea of how 'flow' is achieved will help you to identify a potential source of stress. Is it, for instance, that there is too high a challenge in your working life, and you have not yet attained the skills to meet that challenge? What would you need to do to correct that balance? On the other hand, do you feel frustrated that the skills you have are not being fully utilized? Would more challenge in your working life ease the tension and lift the apathy?

From the many people that Csikszentmihalyi has interviewed there seems no doubt that the experience of 'flow' makes for excellence in life. As he describes it:

> When goals are clear, feedback relevant, and challenges and skills are in balance, attention becomes ordered and fully invested. Because of the total demand on psychic energy, a person in flow is completely focused. There is no space in consciousness for distracting thoughts, irrelevant feelings. Self-consciousness disappears, yet one feels stronger than usual. The sense of time is distorted: hours seem to pass by in minutes. When a person's entire being is stretched in the full functioning of body and mind, whatever one

does becomes worth doing for its own sake; living becomes its own justification. In the harmonious focusing of physical and psychic energy, life finally comes into its own.[16]

You may be able to recognize from that description that you have had an experience of being in 'flow'. You may remember an occasion when your mental and physical abilities were at their height, when there were no emotional distractions because your whole being felt aligned and focused. It may be too much to expect it to be an everyday occurrence, but it would be something to aim for, would it not? And when it happens it would certainly be a good 'state' to anchor, so that you could use the feeling to raise your physical and mental energy when needed (**Habit 2** Pause for Thought 7).

Conclusion

Highly effective teachers know that teaching is a demanding profession that has the potential for generating stress. They recognize the need to maintain mental and physical energy to be able to cope with the demands without resorting to quick-fix short-term solutions such as smoking, drinking too much alcohol or overeating.

The starting-point for developing **Habit 3** is a high level of awareness of the effect of negative stress. This involves:

Physical awareness: Becoming aware of your body and the areas of tension. Listening to what your body is telling you and responding. Recognizing whether your body needs rest and relaxation or exercise and physical stimulation. Building into your lifestyle regular opportunities to conserve and energize your physical resources

Mental awareness: Being able to do a 'reality check' on negative thoughts. Checking whether your thoughts are illogical. Recognizing how negative thoughts can generate stress. Challenging negative thoughts and reframing them into more resourceful mental *re*-presentations

Emotional awareness: Recognizing when emotions are overriding rational responses. Not allowing emotions and worries to grow and drain physical and mental energy, but rather dealing with them in order to get on with life as an empowered professional.

As well as being aware of themselves and their responses, good teachers are able to take action on stress because they have a range of strategies to counter the physical, mental and emotional effects that result from negative stress. They can cope with the mundane and routine part of their work, because they have had the experience of 'flow', and recognize that a demanding profession can also bring moments of highly challenging yet absorbing experiences. Moreover, they can deal swiftly and efficiently with the routine, choosing not to bury themselves in a comfort-blanket of work. They choose to deal with negative thoughts and emotions, rather than let them linger on, so that they can maximize their mental and physical energy to find interest and stimulation in everything around them.

Reflection: Taking time to relax

We all need to make space in our lives to replenish our mental and physical resources. It takes practice to achieve the maximum benefit from a relaxation technique. When you become practised, you find that benefits can be gained from quite a short session.

You need to set aside a time and place where you can be quiet and undisturbed. Make sure you are able to sit comfortably. It may be helpful either to get someone to read these instructions to you, or to tape them and play them back to yourself.

- Begin by checking for any areas of tension in your body.
- Start with your feet, feel your feet resting on the floor. Wriggle your toes and let them rest back in position.
- Now your legs: first check for any muscular tension, then feel the muscles in your calves and thighs become heavy and relaxed.
- Feel your body as you are sitting in the chair. Let your body rest gently down into the seat.
- Now think about your hands and arms. Become aware of how your hands are resting. Stretch your fingers and let them rest back in their position.

- Check for any tension in your arms. As your arms become heavy and relaxed, this will help you to drop your shoulders. Release any tension that's left in your shoulders.
- Move your head gently around so that you can be sure there is no tension in your neck.
- Now think about the muscles of your face. Feel a hand smoothing your brow, smoothing away any tightness. Let your jaw drop so that your mouth relaxes open. Feel your tongue resting in your mouth.
- Now check back over the whole of your body to make sure there are no areas of tension. Feel how pleasurable it is to be sitting relaxed, quiet and calm.
- A last check on your breathing, enjoy the rhythm as your lungs expand to take in air, and release it out again. In–out. In–out. Feel your breathing becoming deeper, each breath increasing your relaxation.

While your body is in this comfortable, relaxed state, you can move to mental relaxation. As you listen to the following passage, you may be able to hear my voice saying the words to you, the quiet tone, the pauses:

And I'm curious to know ... because it's interesting, isn't it ... to notice whether perhaps your life is a little like walking a tightrope.

Because it could be, couldn't it ... that it takes so much control, so much effort, just to stay on the wire. Just to stay balanced ... just to stay on line. I was reading in a book the other day, where someone had said that when someone they knew did this they had to keep their eyes on a fixed point in front of them. And I was wondering ... if you did this ... all your strength going into staying upright and moving ahead ... your eyes focused on one small point ahead ... would you have any awareness of anything going on around you ... or would you not?

It could also be ... couldn't it, that somebody doing this wouldn't be able to look down ... would they? There might be a fear of losing control ... A fear of what was unknown ... of not being able to get back on balance.

It could be ... couldn't it ... that what was below was a plump, jolly bouncy-castle. And that having allowed yourself a momentary relaxation ... the experience *could* be of falling into the cushioned plumpshiousness ... and having done so ... you would be able to bounce away merrily. You would be able to re-experience the physical relaxation of a child ... limbs flopping ... giggling at the sheer fun and effortless relaxation of it all. Able to enjoy the moment completely because you knew that when you chose to, you could bounce back ... up onto the tightrope, back on course.

And I'm curious to know whether ... having allowed yourself to have this experience ... having allowed yourself to enjoy the change ... now with the new learning that there's nothing to fear ... I'm curious to know whether the experience of the tightrope will be the same as before ... or will it be different?

Because it could be ... couldn't it ... that this new relaxation, this new learning, would mean the walk along the tightrope could be accomplished effortlessly ... balanced, upright, confident ... knowing that any time you wanted, you could jump off and re-experience the relaxation and the new learning. Knowing that when you chose, you could bounce back onto the tightrope ready to continue your journey ... gliding and smoothly ... evermore effortlessly with each new learning.

And it's good isn't it, now life is like that?

Give yourself a moment to become aware of your surroundings. Focus on what you can see – where you are sitting, the room, the furniture. Become aware of the sounds you can hear. Notice how your body feels.

When you are ready, move on with what you have to do, refreshed with renewed vigour and energy.

Notes

1. Maxim Gorky 1973.
2. Senge 1990: 367.
3. Open University 1992.

4. Ibid.
5. LeDoux 1998: 302.
6. Ibid., p. 72.
7. Ibid., p. 302.
8. Coe *et al.* 1985: 163-99. Also cited by Barnes *et al.* 1998: 134.
9. *Hamlet*, Act II, ii, 1.
10. See **Habit 2** and Appendix 1.
11. Csikszentmihalyi, 1997: 22.
12. Hare and Reynolds 2004: 172.
13. Csikszentmihalyi, 1997: 17-34.
14. Ibid., p. 30.
15. Ibid., p. 31.
16. Ibid., pp. 31-2.

Habit 4: Taking your time

There's so much to do. And there's never enough time. I feel pressured and hassled all day, every day, seven days a week. I've attended time-management seminars and I've tried half a dozen different planning systems. They've helped some, but I still don't feel I'm living the happy, productive, peaceful life I want to live.[1]

The great theologian St Augustine, when asked to define what time was, found himself puzzled. Until he was asked, he knew exactly what time was. But once asked he had no idea what to say. Time was just there – for the taking.[2]

Nowadays we can hardly avoid 'knowing' the time. Our days are bordered by bus and train times, school bells, lesson timetabling, appointments. Our leisure time is organized in relation to TV and radio scheduling, opening times of shops and leisure centres, cinema showings, match start-times.

We no longer follow the natural change of the days and seasons as did our ancestors. Artificial lighting means that we can turn night into day if we so choose. We no longer measure time by the solstices, and the shortest and longest days have little meaning for us. We even 'adjust' time to fit our needs, as with British Summer Time. Our experience of time, unlike that of our ancestors, is a social construction.

Perhaps more than any other professionals, teachers are subjected to external time pressures. School starts and ends at set times of the day. Learning has to be accomplished during terms that are a set number of weeks. Examinations occur in an annual cycle. Holidays are pre-ordained by local authorities.

Yet even in our time-ordered world, individually our personal experience of time will differ. For myself, I couldn't manage without my diary as the organizer of my time. I like to set myself deadlines for when I have to complete tasks. I have a little notebook in which I jot down things to do and get a great deal of satisfaction as I cross them off when completed. Once I've committed an appointment to my diary I then don't have to worry about it. I generally work backwards from the time when I need to be anywhere, working out how long it will take in order to decide the time I have to leave. I'm always on time for appointments unless something unforeseen occurs. I always check the time a meeting will end as well as when it begins. I allow time to brief myself for meetings, and I always have the right papers with me at a meeting.

On the other hand, when I have a meeting with my colleague Nigel in the coffee-bar at the university I know I can be a little relaxed about when I arrive. Whatever time we arrange to meet, Nigel will generally be late. I'm probably half-way through my first cup of coffee when he rushes in, full of apologies. It will then take him several minutes to sort through his piles of papers to find the ones for our discussion. He was once 45 minutes late because he was so involved in work on his computer that he couldn't drag himself away.

Probably that description is now a little outdated. Over the years Nigel has learned some time-management skills. He has acquired a diary and tried out different methods of recording 'things to do' from colour-coding to A, B, C prioritizing. He now quite likes it when we plan a schedule of work together, and much against his natural inclination, he even manages to stick to our timetable!

It's that 'natural inclination' that is the interesting thing about individual approaches to time-management. Why is it that Nigel and I have very different tendencies that feel right for each of us? Why is it that the old adage 'if you want something done, ask a busy person' still holds true? Why is it that some people never seem to get on top of what they have to do? Why is it that some people achieve the goals they set themselves while others do not?

Habit 5 will give you some strategies for goal-setting and making the best use of your time. But before you can put them into practice and expect to make a change in your life, you need to become aware of your personal perception of time. Because, interestingly enough, although on a daily basis time is the one thing in which we share an equal allowance, how we perceive time is as different and unique to us as our fingerprints.

In this world, there are two times. There is mechanical time and there is body time. The first is as rigid and metallic as a massive pendulum of iron that swings back and forth, back and forth, back and forth. The second squirms and wriggles like a bluefish in a bay. The first is unyielding, predetermined. The second makes up its mind as it goes along.

Many are convinced that mechanical time does not exist ... They wear watches on their wrists, but only as ornaments or as courtesies to those who would give timepieces as gifts. They do not keep clocks in their houses. Instead they listen to their heartbeats. They feel the rhythms of their moods and desires. Such people eat when they are hungry, go to their jobs ... whenever they wake from their sleep, make love all hours of the day. Such people laugh at the thought of mechanical time. They know that time moves in fits and starts. They know that time struggles forward with a weight on its back when they are rushing an injured child to the hospital or bearing the gaze of a neighbour wronged. And they know too that time darts across the field of vision when they are eating well with friends or receiving praise or lying in the arms of a secret lover.

Then there are those who think their bodies don't exist. They live by mechanical time. They rise at seven o'clock in the morning. They eat their lunch at noon and their supper at six. They arrive at their appointments on time, precisely by the clock. They make love between eight and ten at night. They work forty hours a week, read the Sunday paper on Sunday, play chess on Tuesday nights. When their stomach growls, they look at their watch to see if it is time to eat. When they begin to lose themselves in a concert, they look at the clock above the stage to see when it will be time to go home. They know that the body is not a thing of wild magic, but a collection of chemicals, tissues, and nerve impulses. Thoughts are no more than electrical surges in the brain ... The body is a thing to be ordered, not obeyed.

Each time is true, but the truths are not the same.

Figure 9 'Einstein's dreams'
Source: Lightman 1993.

Your personal time-line

Despite the fact that time is universal, our understanding of it is influenced by our culture. There is a view that we developed a certain concept of time in the Western world as a result of the Industrial Revolution, which spawned a need for all the workers to arrive at factories at a certain time, otherwise machines couldn't operate. Assembly-line production enhanced a notion that time was linear, with one thing occurring after another in a sequence of events.[3] Some people also claim there is evidence of the influence of our capitalist heritage in the terms we use to talk about time – budgeting, investing, allocating, wasting,[4] and of course, management and saving.

Warm-climate cultures appear to operate a different notion of time. In the Caribbean and Mexico '*manana*' can mean anything from tomorrow to three weeks from now. Students I have taught who originate from African countries wonder how they will relate back in a business world where appointment times are flexible rather than set.

Cultural factors may be influential, but they do not provide the complete answer to differences in perception of time. If it were the whole answer, then Nigel and I would be more alike as we've always lived and worked in a Western culture. Rather, it's our individual mental *re*-presentation of time that makes the difference, and this difference influences our behaviour. Just as it does with everyone.

The way we *re*-present time is one of the features of our mental map of the world. We have to have a way of knowing the difference between past, present and future, otherwise how would we know the difference? Without checking any factual information, you can recognize mentally which was the class you taught last term, as against the class you taught last year, and yet again the class you taught the year before. You are able to know the difference, and you will know when in the past an event took place. Then again, if you think of yourself teaching next year's class, you will recognize that this is an event in the future. It's an essential aspect of the survival and evolution of the human species that we are able to know the difference between a real event, or an event that is remembered or made up.[5]

Further than this, how we individually encode time has implications for our personal development. Firstly, it does seem that almost everyone stores time in a linear way.[6] Just think about some of the language we use in relation to time. We talk about 'forward-planning', 'looking towards the future', 'time stretching ahead of us' and 'having time on our side'. Then again we refer to 'looking back on things' and 'putting the past behind us'. It's an aspect that has engaged many in philosophical debate.

Secondly, once you recognize how you encode time mentally, you will become aware of how your personal perception of time has a predictable effect on your behaviour.

You may find it quite difficult at first to recognize your particular style of re-presenting time. In considering how you organize time, first think of something in your past and notice the direction the thought came from. Now think of something in the future and again, notice the direction. Now point to past and the future to gain a sense of your personal time-line.

Your perception may align with one of the two major orientations – *through time* or *in time* – or it may be a combination of both. If you pointed behind you for the past, it is likely that you have an *in-time* orientation. If you pointed to your left for the past, your organization could be *through-time*. But don't worry if it's not as clear as that for you. Pause for Thought 9 gives an indication of range of ways that people mentally organize time, which will help you towards identifying your own particular arrangement.

Pause for Thought 9: How do you take time?

Rose had worked in a business environment before training as a teacher. She was ambitious for personal advancement and carried her brisk businesslike approach with her into teaching. She gained promotion in each of the first four years of teaching and soon held a senior-management post. If you asked Rose where the past was for her, she would have no hesitation in gesturing over her shoulder, indicating it was behind her. For Rose, work was something that you got on with as quickly and efficiently as possible. When a colleague told Rose she was still smarting from a sharp comment she had made some time ago, Rose couldn't understand it. For Rose, the past was gone and forgotten and her future progression was more important to her.

When Lois was asked where the past was for her she patted the top of her head. For her, the past was a weight that was pressing down on her, that she was having to carry around with her. Lois always found the work of teaching demanding, and after the birth of her son, the strain became too much for her. She resigned her post to become a full-time mother.

Michael always lived in the moment. His class loved him because he was a relaxed and amusing teacher, although those children who liked to feel secure in where they were going with their work could find his spontaneity a little off-putting. His headteacher despaired of ever getting him to submit lesson-planning on time, if at all. Michael's girlfriend used to say he couldn't see further than his nose. They frequently argued over bills left unpaid because he was unable to anticipate the consequences of not paying them. Indeed, his monthly salary was something to be spent on whatever took his fancy at the time.

I have always been able to 'see' time. For me, events in time are laid out in front of me like a calendar. The past is on my left, with most recent events nearest, then moving away into the far distance. The future in on my right, and the present, where I am now, is immediately in front of me. If I am talking about a time-frame, such as when I'm describing to students the historical development of an education policy, I will tend to gesture with my hands, indicating to the left for past events, and the right for future developments. In the past, my 'natural' time-orientation kept me unhealthily concerned with the past and the future and unable to live 'in the moment'. As a result I suffered stress and depression to the degree that I was unable to work for periods of time. Now that I know how my time-orientation affects my behaviour, I can more easily choose to adopt a different orientation. My clear visual representation of time helps me when I'm involved in planning and estimating the time a piece of work will take. And I now get more enjoyment from both work and leisure because I can change to be 100 per cent in the moment without allowing myself to be distracted by concerns about what happened yesterday, or what will happen tomorrow.

One further point before moving on to some strategies to make best use of your time. Your time-line orientation does not just affect your ability to organize your time, it also influences how involved you are in what you are doing:

- *Disassociated:* With a predominantly *through-time* orientation, people may be doing their work while their mind is on other things. They may be effective at one level, while not being wholly involved in what they are doing at any one time. Thinking about what may have happened yesterday and worrying about what's going to happen tomorrow creates a distraction from the present. Consequently, this orientation can be a source of stress.
- *Associated:* An *in-time* orientation means that people may be 100 per cent involved in what they are doing. Because the past is 'behind them' it does not constitute a distraction to their daily activities. Because they are freed from thinking about the past they can immerse themselves fully in what they are doing at the time. It also means that they may fail to learn from the past and have difficulty planning for the future.

These concepts have no intrinsic value. They are what they are: each orientation has its advantages and disadvantages. They're also not fixed or permanent. Highly effective teachers have been able to recognize how to adapt their time-line thinking preference to improve their time-management behaviour. And you too can do that.

For instance, if you have a term's lesson-planning to produce by a deadline, adopting a through-time orientation will obviously have advantages. You will be able to build on what you have done before, have a sense of what you need to do in the future and be able to get your planning in on time. On the other hand, your class will benefit most from your teaching when you are fully involved in what they are working on at any one time. An *in-time* orientation will enable you to be 'in the moment' in the classroom, enthusiastic and totally aware of everything that is happening.

And when you leave school at the end of the week, being able to shut your classroom door and immerse yourself in activities around home, family or leisure, without being concerned with what happened last week or what will be happening next week, is the best way to maintain a healthy stress-free attitude. Remember: *100 per cent commitment to what you are doing at any one time is a really powerful stress-proofing attitude.*

Switching to an *in-time* orientation will help you gain most from leisure activities. Telling yourself that you can switch back to *through-time* when you need to organize and plan your work will give you the confidence to relax and enjoy the moment.

Procrastination

Understanding how you experience time and your time-line preference will have the first major effect on your time-management. However, at a practical level, you will still need to deal with everyday tasks – those tasks that you keep putting off but which at the same time you *know* you should be doing.

We all procrastinate – and, as the saying goes, procrastination is the thief of time. I don't particularly like housework, but when I was a student my house was the cleanest it had ever been. I would resort to any household cleaning task rather than get down to writing the essay I needed to be working on. For one of my fellow students her distraction activity was grooming her cat. For both of us, 100 per cent mediocre activity was better than getting down to the task in hand. And most annoying – once I'd got started on the essay I'd been putting off, I found it wasn't as difficult as I thought, and I wished I'd started earlier!

You may recognize the sort of excuses you make to yourself: how you convince yourself you have very good reasons for *not* doing that essential task. The trouble is, when we play games with ourselves to find good reasons why we should not get on with something, we drain our psychic energy. William James put it succinctly: 'Nothing is so fatiguing as the eternal hanging-on of an uncompleted task.'[7] I'd be a wealthy woman if I'd saved a pound every time I heard a student say 'I only start an essay at the last minute because I work best under pressure.' And it's not just students: I've had this said to me by senior managers who put off major pieces of work and then work into the early hours to meet a deadline. In both cases, because their outcome has generally been satisfactory, they've been able to convince themselves that this is their best way of working. The reality is that there are often more mistakes in rushed work and no time to correct them. In this approach, the motivation has been the looming deadline, rather than a motivation to do their best work. So they continue putting themselves under stress, oblivious to whether trying another method would actually make life easier for them and those around them – as well as having the potential to achieve an outcome that really was their best work, not just a satisfactory attempt.

This is not to deny that important pieces of work need an incubation period to allow creative thoughts to formulate. But time-management techniques apply to thinking-time as well. If it's a report or essay of some kind, you need to make a realistic estimate of the time it will take to write it, and set yourself a date and time when you will start. Then before you reach the time to start writing you can schedule the times you will be gathering your research, making notes, formulating an outline. It doesn't have to be formal time – I always have some reading that will trigger my thought processes during a train journey. Throughout all these activities your unconscious mind will be incubating your ideas so that once you start to write you will have done your thinking preparation and will be more likely to produce your best work. This is a lot better than condensing the writing and thinking together which puts you under pressure and can be anxiety-provoking.

Pause for Thought 10: Procrastination game plan

Excuse	Response
I don't like doing this task	Find something that you *do* take pleasure in to get you started, e.g. keep favourite pen to do your marking, so that thinking about the pleasure of using it will get you started.
	Reframe your self-talk from 'don't like' and tell yourself what part of the task you *do* like.
	Plan the reward you are going to give yourself when you've finished.
	Give yourself a tight time-frame and say that you'll finish in time to leave school at a certain time, watch your favourite TV programme, have a cup of coffee, or go out with friends.

This task is so big I don't know where to start	Use the 'salami' approach – slice it up. Start on a small part, not necessarily the beginning, but start somewhere. Even better, do the worst first.
I don't know how to do this task	Accept that you need to ask for help. Ask for the assistance you need and do it now!
I need more information before I start	Go and find it!
I'm too busy	What will it cost to put it off? Will other people suffer if you don't do it? How are you likely to feel if you don't do it? Will you have to rush to complete it at a later time and do an inferior job? How will you feel about that? Make a realistic judgement on your workload. If you really consider you have too much to do compared with other people, ask your line manager how she wants you to prioritize. If necessary, ask if other people can be involved to help you with the task.

Remember: Moving friction is greater than starting friction. The most important thing is to START SOMEWHERE

Prioritizing: finding what's important for you

The biggest motivator to overcome the delaying tactics of procrastination is having a clear sense of what's important to you and what you are aiming for in life. Highly effective teachers take time to think through what's important about their work so that they don't waste time on unimportant things.

At a basic level, it's about defining your response to what's *urgent*, as against what's *important*. Urgent matters are those that demand our immediate attention. They're the matters that take up our time when we fill our days with busy work, dashing around reacting to crises or problems. Important matters are not so visible, but they're the matters where we can be proactive in working towards our long-term goals, the matters that ensure job-satisfaction and empowerment.

If you fill your time reacting to things that need urgent attention, then you will probably be considered very *efficient*. But if you are assuming these urgent matters are also important, you are not being as *effective* as you could be. Think about it this way – say I held a wad of banknotes in my hand and threw them into the air and invited people to grab them. The person who rushed around grabbing as many notes as possible would certainly be the most *efficient* person – but the person who went straight for the single £50 note would be the most *effective*.

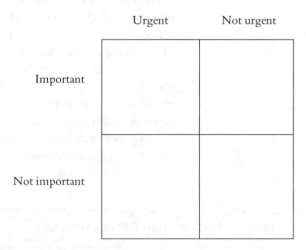

Figure 10   Urgent/important matrix 1
Source: Adapted from Covey 1992.

You can define for yourself how you involve yourself in *urgent* and *important* matters by using the matrix in Figure 10. This suggests you can sort matters that need your attention into four distinct categories:

Urgent and not important: These are things that demand your immediate attention. If the phone rings for instance, most people would just *have* to answer it. Some people can be deceived into believing that reacting to urgent matters is doing important work. The reality is that the urgency can be based on other people's priorities and expectations. When people are struggling to meet the demands of the workplace, this is the area where it is tempting to spend most time. But this is the area of crisis-management and fire-fighting, and spending most working time here can lead to burn-out.

Not urgent and not important: When people get overwhelmed by spending most of their working time on urgent/not important matters they can easily slip into the relief of a routine of dealing only with the mundane. Crisis-management takes its toll in depleted physical and mental energy so that teaching can become no more than a series of routinized actions.

Not urgent but important: This is the area of things that we know are important but may find difficulty getting round to doing. They are the activities that are the building blocks of an empowered professional. They include things like building relationships, long-term planning, health-maintenance, planning and preparation, crisis-prevention. Highly effective teachers make sure they allocate time to focus on those activities that will contribute to building their capacity for long-term achievements.

Urgent and important: Identifying what's important and paying attention to it will leave the matters in this last category comparatively small. Highly effective teachers recognize and deal swiftly with matters in this category. Taking the time to build a relationship with a class, for instance, will reduce the incidence of disruptive behaviour. Once disruptive behaviour is thought of as urgent but not important, it will be dealt with swiftly and effectively, rather than allowing it to assume an unnecessary importance.

Dealing with your own activities as suggested in Figure 11 will have two important effects. Making sure your main focus is on *important/not urgent* matters ensures empowerment. Taking preventative action by making sure *important* matters are not neglected will reduce the incidence of matters needing your immediate attention. Applying the *urgent/important* test may actually reduce what you have to do to a quarter of what you *thought* you had to do!

	Urgent	Not urgent
Important	**DO IT NOW!**	**PLAN IT**
Not important	**DELEGATE IT**	**LEAVE IT**

Figure 11   Urgent/important matrix 2
Source: Adapted from Covey 1992.

Creating achievable outcomes

Many people give up on the whole idea of goal-setting and planning for outcomes because they never achieve what they set out to do. 'The best-laid plans . . .' they will often quote, as if some external force is bent on interfering with their plans and thwarting their goals.

These people may also be very scathing about others who do achieve success. They may put it down to luck, to being in the right place at the right time, to being 'in the know' in some way. Because their own plans never come to fruition, they conclude that other people's success must come down to some external advantage that they themselves haven't been able to acquire.

What they fail to recognize is that people who are successful in what they do are usually very clear about what's important to them, and they have set themselves positive outcomes to aim for. Although they are clear about their outcomes, they are also flexible enough to adjust their plans in light of events, rather than sticking rigidly to a plan then bemoaning its failure. Because they've taken the time to think through their objectives, they have put themselves in a position to take advantage of opportunities when they arise. They are able to make their own luck.

One way to check out the viability of goals you set yourself is to apply the SMART test. You can check whether your objective is worded in such a way that it meets the requirements for achievement. Is it

- Specific
- Measurable
- Achievable
- Realistic
- Time-related?

An objective to 'improve the performance of my class in examinations' would not meet the SMART test. Whereas a goal to 'increase the number of pupils in my class achieving Grade 5 in this year's SATs by 25 per cent' would meet the criteria. If you're setting a goal, you have to be able to have a measure of having achieved it.

But even when people achieve the goals they've set themselves, it may in some cases seem a hollow victory. Remember Gaynor whom I described in **Habit 3**? She pursued promotion because she thought it was the Crustimoney Proseedcake – the Thing to Do. Yet she ended up being thoroughly miserable and unable to gain any satisfaction from achieving her goal.

Thus there is a lot more to being a highly effective teacher than setting objectives that meet the SMART criteria, or aiming for something you think you *should* or *ought* to be aiming for. A vision of a goal that has been thought through, that fits with your values, that is framed in realistic, positive terms, can be so seductive that it *propels* you toward it, almost despite yourself. Your vision needs to be such, that when you think about it, you experience a surge of excitement and energy that is compelling and irresistible.

Take a step towards that vision now:

- Ask yourself what you would like to be doing next year, in five years.
- Think about what's important to you about teaching (see in Introduction, p. 10).
- How will your vision fit with your values about teaching?
- Can you be sure that your vision would not be dependent upon other people?

- Resist the temptation to think in terms of what you should/ought/must be doing; your vision needs to be what you really want for yourself.

Now use Pause for Thought 11 to create a mental re-presentation of your vision.

Pause for Thought 11: The mighty acorn and the tiny oak tree[8]

Mighty oaks from little acorns grow

Most people are familiar with the proverb above, but have you ever really considered what a powerful metaphor it is for the way in which we can achieve the results we want in life?

Many people go for goals with no clear structure, or without checking the overall effect of the goal. When this happens, they can often find that the goal wasn't what they really wanted after all. Using our acorn metaphor, it would be pretty silly to plant pine cones and expect an oak tree to grow. It wouldn't make much sense to plant an oak tree in the desert and expect it to survive without help. Neither would you expect a hundred acorns planted in the same six-foot square plot to all survive as oak trees. And if you planted an acorn tonight it would be unrealistic to look out of your window expecting to see an oak tree the next day.

Yet in some way, these are all the kinds of things people do in relation to achieving results, even though common sense tells us that they're unrealistic.

After all, the fully grown oak tree may look mighty, but in many ways it's actually the acorn that's more impressive. Without the acorn, the oak would never exist. And the acorn has had to overcome many obstacles on the path to becoming an oak.

So the **ACORN** acronym is useful for checking you have all the pieces in place to ensure that you also get the results you want. It contains all the essential pieces and questions to ensure that you achieve results effectively and ecologically.

At any stage you may decide to modify, change or abandon the initial goal you have thought of – and that's OK. Many people waste time going for pipe-dreams, fantasies and unrealistic and unachievable results. This model should ensure that you actually get what you go for!

Act as if you have already achieved the result. In other words, let's pretend you have already achieved what you are going for and then answer these questions:

- What are you seeing and hearing and feeling?
- What set of words accurately describes in a positive way what you have achieved? (Check that these do not include negatives like 'I'm not stressed anymore' or 'there's no problem any more' – because the brain cannot think about *not* wanting something without first thinking about the very thing you don't want! Say what you want, not what you don't want.)

Check the effects of achieving this.

- Having achieved your goal, how does it affect you?
- How else does it affect you ...?
- And what does that mean for you?
- What are the effects on other people – friends, family, work colleagues, etc.?
- What other effects might there be and what are the implications?

(Before moving on you may need to go back to **Acting as if** to see, hear and feel if the goal you are going for has changed.)

Ownership of the goal

After answering all of these questions, is the goal something you still want? Can you say, hand on heart, that after truthfully answering the questions above you are 100 per cent committed to this.

Can you personally begin and maintain the necessary actions that are needed to achieve the goal (this doesn't mean you have to do everything yourself – but it does mean you have to have the power and authority to control the key elements).

If you can't say 'yes' to all of these, then you need to go back to **Acting as if** and reassess the goal. Or maybe go for another goal instead.

Resources

- What resources do you already have in terms of time, materials, people and money?
- What resources can you acquire, and from where and whom?
- Do you need any new resources in terms of skills or behaviours for yourself or others?

At this stage you may find yourself breaking down the result you are going for into a series of smaller things, all of which can be put through the same **Acorn** process.

Now do it!
Create the detailed action plan and *take the first step now!*

Achieving work–life balance

The approach to 'time -management' in **Habit 4** is not about making it possible to do more in the time available. Rather, it starts with understanding yourself and your relationship with time. Gaining that sort of understanding will help you towards the *real* aim of time-management – achieving a good work–life balance.

Part of understanding yourself is discovering your 'prime time'. Your prime time is that part of the day when you regularly feel more energized and capable. It's the time to schedule those tasks that you usually procrastinate over or the really important stuff that you want to do well. Many years ago when I was teaching and following a masters degree at the same time, I found the only way I could get essays written was to get up early before the rest of the family. I discovered that my concentration was best at 5.00 a.m., and I achieved much more then with seemingly less effort than when I struggled with tiredness and distractions. I'm still an early riser (although not always as early as 5.00 a.m.) because I know that's when I'm at my most productive.

Your own prime time may be a different time of day, and if you think about when it is, you'll probably realize there is also a time of day when your energy dips. That will obviously be the time to avoid so far as attempting serious work is concerned. Struggling against your natural bodily rhythms will drain your energy and be counter-productive in the long term. Far better in the short term to listen to what your body is telling you – maximizing your prime-time potential and minimizing the effects of your least productive time of day.

Keeping a balance in your life also means scheduling in time for physical and mental energy renewal. It's not just the world that needs sustainable resources, we need to sustain our own energy resources and maintain our sanity in the midst of stressful and often conflicting demands. 'Stability-zones' are those times and things that allow us periods of recovery activity.[9]

A stability-zone can be anything that helps you stay anchored in the storm-tossed sea of your working life. It can be as small as a photograph of a holiday or someone you are fond of – any photograph that gives you a warm feeling when you look at it. Or it could be a poster that you put up on your classroom-wall that brings a sense of peace and calm to the room. A stability-zone can be something very practical that you do: something that you can immerse yourself in to take your mind off things, such as going to the gym, cooking, a hobby. A stability-zone can also be the time you spend with people you love and friends whose company you enjoy. People who are always there for you, who keep you grounded; people who when you're with them you feel you can just be yourself. A stability-zone can also be something less tangible, but which nevertheless keeps you grounded: your values and beliefs, the professional and personal standards you want to live up to.

Highly effective teachers ensure they have enough stability-zones to help them achieve work–life balance. Thinking about the balance in your life is well worth the investment of time that it will take. You can do this with Pause for Thought 12: think about the things in your life that act as stability-zones for you, then divide up the pie chart according to how important they are to you. You may be led to thinking that there would be benefit for you to add to some areas: friends for instance – how good are you at maintaining networks of people in whose company you feel relaxed? Or places: is there a favourite place that you haven't visited for a long while because you've felt you haven't had the time?

Pause for Thought 12: Your stability-zones

Your values, beliefs, philosophy   . . . .
. . . .
. . . .
. . . .
. . . .

Your activities   . . . .
. . . .
. . . .
. . . .
. . . .
. . . .

Your organizations   . . . .
. . . .
. . . .
. . . .
. . . .

Your places   . . . .
. . . .
. . . .
. . . .
. . . .

Your objects   . . . .
. . . .
. . . .
. . . .
. . . .

Your people   . . . .
. . . .
. . . .
. . . .
. . . .

Now divide the circle in slices that show the importance of the
different types of stability-zone to you at present.

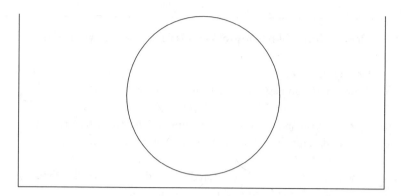

Conclusion

Habit 4 is about taking control of your life and work so that you do the things that are important – with enough spare time to evaluate how you are doing. **Habit 4** does not just attach importance to work-tasks, it includes those activities that you need to undertake to maintain your health and fitness and keep you mentally alert and engaged with the world around you.

Traditional time-management training will give you plenty of tips and strategies to 'save' time. It's true that many people can benefit from time-management training; they may enthuse about it and plunge into using the strategies straight away. And it's also true that after a week or so, many will think that the strategies are not working and will give up and return to their previous ways.

The starting-point for **Habit 4** has been the 'natural' inclination that we appear to have as individuals towards time. We have our own unique way of knowing that the past is the past and the future is the future. Before we can adopt the tips and strategies with any degree of success, we need to understand how our personal *re*-presentation of time affects our time-management behaviour.

Highly effective teachers recognize that time is a resource like any other, and that there is choice in how to spend the time they have. They are able to prioritize, so the important things get done; they have worked out a game-plan that enables them to avoid procrastinating over tasks that may appear tiresome. They can maximize their effectiveness by making best use of their prime time to tackle the important matters. Most importantly, they use their understanding of time to achieve work–life balance and so empower themselves professionally.

Reflection: Neuro-logical levels for time-management

Environment
Take a fresh look at your work environment.

- Do you spend unnecessary time having to move around desks and chairs? Would a different arrangement save you time?
- Is it time you de-cluttered your desk to avoid rifling through papers to find the one you want?
- How effective is your filing system? How long does it take you to find what you want?
- Is your classroom organized so that pupils can find what they need without repeatedly asking you?

Behaviour
- What do you do that 'wastes' time?
- Do you understand the reason you procrastinate and put things off?
- Do you have a strategy to overcome procrastination?
- Do you make 'to-do' lists?
- Are you able to work through your lists once you've made them?

Capability
- Do you *prioritize* the items on your to-do list?
- Do you know your 'prime' time (the time of day when you work best)?
- How do you make best use of your 'prime' time?
- Do you forward-plan to achieve goals that are important to you?

Beliefs and values
- Have you checked that your goals fit with your values?
- Can you tell the difference between what is urgent and what is important?
- Do you use the Pareto Principle to assess your work? (The 80–20 rule: 80 per cent of the value comes from 20 per cent

of the work, therefore concentrating on the most important 20 per cent can improve your work.)

- Do you value yourself sufficiently that you don't allow
  your goals to be sidetracked by unnecessary distractions?
- Do you value yourself enough to give time and attention
  to your health and fitness?

Identity

- Do you know that what you're doing is right for you?
- Are the goals you've set yourself the right goals for you?
- What are your strengths and weaknesses in respect of
  managing time?
- How can you overcome any weaknesses – what ways
  would suit you?

Notes

1. Cited in Covey 1992.
2. Solomon Flores 2001.
3. James and Woodsmall, 1988: 17.
4. Csikszentmihalyi 1997: 8.
5. Hall 1984.
6. James and Woodsmall 1988: 16.
7. William James, *The Letters* on http://www.des.emory.edu/mfp/james
8. Acknowledgement to Stenhouse Consulting for permission to use their
   original model.
9. Concept of 'prime time' and 'stability-zones' taken from Open University 1992.

Part II

Engaging with Others

Habit 5: Establishing creative rapport

For any meaningful interplay of conscious and subconscious, practice is essential.[1]

Habit 5 is about making connections. We all know how it feels to 'connect' to other people. These are the people with whom conversation flows freely, there are no misunderstandings, we feel at ease and there's a sense of trust between us. Sometimes this just seems to happen without any effort on our part so that we assume that some people are more likeable, more easygoing, trustworthy, and that others are just 'difficult'.

Certainly, with some people, making a connection can be a challenge. As, for instance, when you are facing a class of disaffected teenagers, dealing with a parent who disapproves of your teaching approach, or trying to work harmoniously with a colleague who always sees the negative side of everything. Being unable to get along with people in these situations is disconcerting and can be a source of frustration. It's not surprising there's a lot of use of *dis* in describing these irksome situations: my dictionary gives definitions of the prefix *dis* as meaning 'not' or 'a reversal'. In making connections, we are aiming to get rid of the 'not' signified by the *dis* and revert to the original: 'affection', 'agreement', 'approval', working 'in concert'.

Highly effective teachers recognize that the first step in making connections where there is affection, approval and agreement is establishing a *rapport*. Sue Knight has put it succinctly. Rapport is indeed 'a prerequisite to good communication, influence and change'.[2] Whether you're working with students, parents or colleagues, it's the bottom-line essential element of good working relationships. Establishing rapport is firstly a *process*: it's ongoing, dynamic and can change. Secondly, rapport is not something that is neutral, in itself it is *influential*. And thirdly, although rapport seems just to happen with some people, the important thing to realize is that it can be created – you can be *creative* in establishing rapport.

If rapport appears 'just to happen' with some people, because rapport is a process something must be happening between people to create it. It therefore also follows that if rapport is absent, the 'something' that happens to create it must be missing. When our relationships with people are good, although we recognize they are good, we are not always consciously aware of what is happening between us that creates the rapport. A good relationship just seems to happen without any conscious effort on our part. Yet if we can become aware of what is happening in good relationships, we can *empower* ourselves to recreate those good relationships with other people with whom we need to work more harmoniously.

Adopting **Habit 5** means practising the behaviours that create rapport. It means bringing to conscious awareness things that seem to happen intuitively when people fall easily into 'physical and conversational harmony'.[3] It means making the unconscious conscious so that you can discover how much creative ability you already have to empower yourself and others.

Making the unconscious conscious

Let's start with a simple test.

Give yourself 10 seconds only to read the following sentence and count how many f's are in the sentence. Do it quickly then read on:

> Finished files are the result of years of scientific study combined with the experience of years

How many f's did you count? In training sessions there will be a range of answers from delegates, with the majority always opting for three. So if you really did read it quickly, it's likely you would have decided there were two and three f's in the sentence. Perhaps one delegate in a training group will say 'six' – which is the right answer.

If your answer was anything less than six, read it again – did you count the f in 'scientific' and the f's at the end of the three 'ofs'?

This simple test provides an illustration of how we consciously blank-out information that is there all the time. Perhaps because of preconceived ideas, or what we have been conditioned to expect. In this test, the first two f's at the beginning of words are obvious, which sets up an expectation for the rest of the sentence. So when the sentence is scanned swiftly, the f's that occur in the middle and at the end of words can go unnoticed.

It's the same sort of 'blind-spot' I talked about in **Habit 2**. The game of 'Hunt the Thimble' depended upon the fact that in our normal functioning we don't register at a conscious level a great deal of information that is readily available to us. **Habit 2** was a challenge to notice what you notice more carefully, not to make assumptions about what you are seeing, hearing and sensing. To stretch your sensory acuity so that we can be switched on to more subtle messages in other people's verbal and non-verbal communication. Not surprisingly, this raised awareness provides the basis for being creative with rapport. When we can see more, hear more and sense more we have real evidence on which to base good relationships rather than making interpretations from our own mental map. We have more chance of connecting with other people if we try to enter their map of reality instead of expecting them to navigate our own map.[4]

We may not even notice the outward signs indicating that someone is in a particular frame of mind, because of the mental mechanisms that we have developed to cope with the immense amount of information available from our senses (see Figure 12). We may hear the words that someone says to us, but miss the underlying message being conveyed in the intonation. And we may not get close to the essence of another person because we stick in our own sense of self – and our own map – and ignore the potential to 'reach out' and understand what it's really like to be another person. Good teachers are alert to the range of messages from other people; they can create rapport and establish relationships, even when another person's behaviour is challenging and obstructive.

Before moving on to the 'how to' of creating rapport, we need to recognize that there are different levels of rapport. There's a difference between the rapport you need for good working relationships with colleagues, and the rapport you will have with a partner, who may be a soulmate. Getting the level right is important – otherwise you'll be investing a great deal of effort to achieve a deeper level of rapport than is necessary. Not only more than is necessary – it could have unexpected results!

There's an experience of mine that comes to mind whenever I want to stress how the influence of rapport is not to be underestimated.

We have so much information available from our senses – what we can see, hear, touch, taste, smell and sense – that we have evolved mental mechanisms to sort the information, and to select what we pay attention to at any one time. There are three main processes:[5]

Deletion: As you will have noticed from the Finished Files test, if we direct attention at one thing, we can ignore something else. We may not 'see' something that is right in front of our eyes (as in Figure 3), or we may 'tune-out' the chatter in a classroom to listen to the conversation between two particular students. We may also be so immersed in a task that we can be totally unaware of the feelings of another person, or of their reaction to our behaviour. Probably a common example of deletion that most people will have experienced will be thinking about something else while driving, then later having no recollection whatsoever of a part of the journey. Psychologists have referred to human beings as *cognitive misers* in using the process of deletion; it's an efficient strategy for making good use of our limited cognitive capacity to process a near-infinite world of information.[6]

Distortion: With this mechanism we mentally *change* information about the external environment. All artistic creations, all great literature, have come about because the artist or writer has been able to distort and reconfigure present reality. Similarly, advances in science involve the ability to distort and misrepresent existing knowledge and reality.[7] At a more mundane level, if we are involved in interior decorating, we will look at a room and distort our image by imagining what it would look like in a different colour. And psychologists also claim that this process of distortion is nearly universal in the spread of rumours. The spreading of a story, or the recollection of an event some time after is has passed, show similar patterns: while all but a few details will be dropped, at the same time certain details are also sharpened.[8] Distortion is also the mechanism that leads to our tendency to 'mind-read' other people's intentions or meanings, interpreting them from our own mental map rather than checking on the accuracy of what we see and hear.

Generalization: Our ability to *generalize* is an essential mechanism. If we weren't able to do this, every day would present us with a completely new experience. It's one of the ways in which we learn about the world: we draw broad conclusions based on one or more experiences While it's an essential process to avoid having to approach each new experience afresh, it's also the process that causes us to stereotype other people and their behaviour. We may categorize people on the basis of one or two experiences, and our prejudgement then influences how we deal with new people whom we fit into our existing generalizations.

Figure 12 Thinking processes

Some years ago I was on a training course where we were required to work in a team over three days to achieve a task. Right from the start it was evident that one member of our team had not read the briefing papers in advance of the course. While the rest of us were prepared to plunge straight into the task, she attempted delaying tactics to enable her to catch up. Unfortunately, her tactics were perceived as being openly obstructive, and only served to alienate the other team-members. They opted to ignore her, but as one of the outcomes for the training was to analyse how we developed and worked as a team, I decided I wanted to address the challenge of involving her. So I set myself a personal task of building rapport with her – and over two days I worked hard at it. It's a subtle process, so the other members of the team were unaware that anything was happening, but by the time we got to Day 3, there was a very distinct change. For one thing, she had attached herself to me! She sought me out at coffee and lunch breaks, and every time we moved to a different room, she made a point of sitting next to me. But apart from this, and more importantly, her whole attitude calmed over the three days. By the time we got to the final plenary debriefing, she felt able to admit to the group that she recognized her initial behaviour had been defensive because she had arrived unprepared for the task.

I did wonder what the outcome would have been if I hadn't created rapport with her, if I had gone along with the others and ignored her. I felt I learned from this experience that rapport alone can influence an outcome. There has even been the suggestion that most business decisions are made on the basis of rapport rather than on technical merit.[9] In my example, the focus on establishing rapport led to a better outcome, both for the individual and the team. And the fact that I also acquired a 'groupie' is an indicator that creating rapport can have unintended side-effects.

Creating rapport, step 1: matching body-language

There's actually nothing very difficult about creating rapport. We are all able to do it unconsciously. To do it consciously just needs a heightened awareness – a sharpened sensory acuity – and some practice.

The basis of all the steps to creating rapport is the fact that we tend to respond to people who are somewhat like ourselves. We will feel an affinity for someone when we recognize that they think like us, that they like the things we like, that they hold similar values to our own.

So turning that around, if we can indicate an affinity for other people, we are likely to establish rapport. There's a Native American saying that provides a useful metaphor for understanding how to create rapport. It advises: 'To understand a man, you have to walk a mile in his moccasins.' It suggests we need to get a feel for someone else, to put ourselves in their position. Step 1 describes the quick and easy way of doing this: by *matching* something about the other person's physical demeanour we can take a first step into their moccasins.

You can choose to match any single aspect of another person's physical behaviour (see Figure 13). It's what happens anyway when people are in rapport. If you glance around a crowded bar you will know instinctively which people are getting along well. They may sit in a similar manner, cross and uncross their arms or legs at the same time, and their movements may have a natural rhythm, almost as if they were joined in a dance.

> Matching is what we do unconsciously when we get along with people anyway, and with a sharpened sensory acuity we can do it consciously whenever we need to create a climate of trust with another person. So with your new extended sensory acuity to notice more about other people, practise matching one of the following:

Posture: Notice the way the person is sitting or standing, how their weight is distributed. Just as we would naturally sit if another person were sitting rather than stand over them, you can adjust your posture in more subtle ways to create rapport. You may notice a particular inclination of the head, or how the shoulders are held. It's almost routine with me now that the first thing I do in an interview is to notice how a person is seated and settle myself into a matching position.

Sometimes people say to me that they find matching posture difficult if it takes them out of their normal comfortable style. But we only feel comfortable in the way we do things – whether it's the way we sit, stand, move or talk – because it's become a habit to do it that way. As with all our patterns of behaviour, we acquired the habit of behaving the way we do, and we practised until our patterns became so familiar that they seemed to be an irrevocable part of us. But if it means we can get an improved relationship by doing things another way, then we can learn to do that also. It can seem strange at first to step outside your own comfort-zone, but if flexibility means a working relationship can be improved, it's definitely worth a little practice.

Gestures and movements: Notice the way a person holds their arms and whether they use particular gestures. If the other person makes rather flamboyant movements of the arms it would be very obvious to attempt to match exactly. However, you can make smaller matching movements with just a hand, or even with fingers. This can be particularly effective when summarizing what someone has said to check you have understood the meaning. If you repeat the gestures along with the words, not only will you be conveying a strong impression that you understand what they have been saying, you really *will* understand because you will be *matching* their experience.

Voice: There is so much about the voice that you can choose to match: it could be the volume, the speed of speech, the intonation. Done well, it can be a very effective method of creating rapport. I remember a visit a colleague and I made to a database expert, when we needed to find out how particular information was stored. The expert was a techie with a particular clipped way of speaking – his sentences came in short sharp bursts as though fired from a machine gun. Every time we asked a question, the answer shot back in technological shorthand, without the fuller explanations we needed. Then I realized that what had started as a three-way interview was evolving into a two-way conversation. He was directing his explanations more to my colleague than myself, and she was managing to get him to respond to questioning and fill in the details we needed. As she was doing much better than I was, I sat back and let the conversation flow. It was then I noticed what was happening. She had slipped into matching his mode of speech exactly – speed of delivery, shortness of sentences, volume. It was a masterclass on how to establish rapport by voice matching – and she was completely unaware of her expertise!

A similar example was described to me in a training session. A delegate who was a clinic nurse mentioned how she had been impressed by a consultant she had worked for, because of her flexibility when speaking to patients. Over the course of a day, this physician saw many patients, and the nurse noticed she responded to each one by matching their manner of speech. It was noticeable to the nurse, because she was there throughout the day, but for each individual patient they were only aware that they were being treated in a manner that respected their individuality.

Breathing: Perhaps the most difficult when you first try matching, this can also be the most powerful. It's not a new idea that when people are in close affinity they may also be breathing in unison: our word 'conspirator' is derived from the Latin that originally meant 'to breathe with'. Assessing a person's breathing-rate can be a challenge at first – staring at another person's chest would probably not be the most polite thing to do – there are more subtle ways to aim to match breathing. The speed of a person's speech is a good indicator, and looking for any rise and fall of their shoulders can give a sense of their rate of breathing. Since a person's mood or state will affect their breathing, being able to match at this level is a very powerful route to understanding their experience.

Figure 13   Creating rapport by body-matching

When you set out to body-match, just because you will be matching deliberately doesn't mean it will be mimicry or copying. Rather, the underlying motivation needs to be to create understanding and a climate of trust. Body-matching should be done respectfully, with care and subtlety. And if it's done subtly and elegantly the other person will be unaware that anything deliberate is happening.

There have been many times in training when I've described the principle of matching and a particular delegate has responded, 'Oh, I'm quite sure a patient/client/student would notice if I did that.' Then we run a practice exercise, and invariably that same person will be completely unaware that another delegate has been deliberating matching an aspect of their physical behaviour.

Walking in someone else's shoes (or moccasins) is a useful metaphor for understanding the simplest and quickest way to build rapport. It quite literally could be a first step, as in the example of trying to maintain a conversation with someone while walking along a corridor, or a street. The chances are, if you're getting along, at the same time as you're interacting verbally, you'll be pacing yourself so that you walk in time with each other. Even the phrase I've just used – *getting along* – suggests that this is what we do. (And the reverse is also true; I have a colleague who always strides ahead of everyone else, maintaining a conversation over his shoulder. I usually end up a few feet behind him, gasping for breath as I try to keep up and converse at the same time. If you've had a similar experience, think about how it feels to be *mis*matched that way.)

Pause for Thought 13: Resistance in another person is a sign of lack of rapport[10]

When Richard was a primary school headteacher he was called one day to help with a situation in a classroom. David was a little boy in the Reception class who used a particular strategy when he was disinclined to join in with the class activities. He would crawl under the nearest convenient table or chair and resist all attempts to entice him out. On this particular day, David had crawled under a low bench and, despite the urging of two teachers, refused to emerge. The rest of the class had moved into the hall for their next activity, and, not wishing to pull him out physically, the teachers asked Richard for his help. Richard assessed the situation, aware that two teachers had already tried all inducements they could think of, and decided to give the inconceivable a try. He lay down beside David on the cold stone floor. The bench was too low for Richard to join the small boy under it, but he lay as close beside him as he could, matching his body posture. The pair lay there together, Richard looking at David and matching his breathing. Time passed – Richard was not sure how long – but once he intuitively felt a connection had been established, he made his next move. 'I'm not very comfortable here,' he said to David, 'and I'm getting cold. So I'm going to get up now.' Richard rose to his feet. Without a word, David crawled out from under the bench and stood beside him. Richard took his hand and together they walked calmly and quietly into the hall to join the rest of the class.

Creating rapport, step 2: Matching language

As your ability to notice more and more about other people develops, you will recognize more and more how different people are. You will notice how we all have unique features in how we use our bodies: the habitual gestures that one person makes, the way another person always sits at their desk, the elements of another person's voice that are always the same but that you hadn't noticed before.

The same will apply to the language that people use. We may all speak the same basic language, but we will all have our own unique way of using the words. And the choice of words and phrases a person uses provides a further opportunity to create rapport by getting close to their way of thinking.

If you have adopted **Habit 1** you will have been more aware of your own thinking comfort-zone. You will have noticed whether you have a preference for thinking in pictures, thinking through sounds, processing through feelings, or predominantly talking to yourself. As you become aware that your own way of thinking and learning is unique, you will become able to recognize that other people have different thinking comfort-zones. You can develop your awareness further by recognizing that we all give clues to our own way of thinking in the language we use. Which gives us a further

Visual

If I could show you a really brilliant way of communicating, that could make you appear more attractive to visionary people, you would at least want to look at it, wouldn't you?

The benefits of creating rapport with people who have a preference for visual processing is that it would become so much clearer to see the way people view the world. It is when you see how things look from other points of view that you catch sight of the bigger picture. From this perspective it is easier to see the way forward to a really bright future for everyone.

Auditory

If I were to tell you about a way of communicating with people that would really want to make them prick up their ears and listen, you would at least want to hear about it, wouldn't you?

Striking a harmonious chord with someone with an auditory preference might sound easy to you. Being in tune with someone means that you are talking their language. The language that you speak can create sweet music and orchestrate a whole group.

Kinaesthetic

If I were to give you a really concrete way to get in touch with people, so that you can build rapport at a really deep level and get to grips with the way they hold reality, you would at least want to get a feel for it, wouldn't you?

When you find common ground with people you may feel things moving along more smoothly, find new connections are made and that the path ahead becomes a stroll in the park.

Unspecified

If I were to invite you to consider the idea that some people process their understandings of the work in a very distinct and precise manner, is this a concept that might intrigue you?

Knowing how people think can help you expand your perception and it is a very effective way to learn the answers to some of those questions which cross your mind from time to time. It might even change the way you communicate with people depending on what sense you can make of them.

Figure 14   Creating rapport by matching language patterns
Source: Stenhouse Consulting.

opportunity to create rapport – we can match the language patterns that we notice people using.

For instance, a person who is thinking in pictures will be likely to use phrases such as 'I see what you mean', 'I'm glad we see eye to eye', 'That's not clear to me, I need to see it in black and white.' Conversely, a person who is thinking in sounds or hearing an internal voice may use phrases such as 'I hear you loud and clear', 'Can we talk this over?' 'It seems like a good idea, but something tells me it won't work.' And a person who thinks in terms of feelings is likely to use phrases such as 'It's been weighing on my mind', 'I can't grasp the issues here', 'Let's walk this through step by step.'

Where people don't seem to be demonstrating a preference for a sensory-specific thinking pattern, this may be recognized in their *unspecified* language; their use of words such as 'prove', 'plan', 'know', 'discover'. However, make no mistake, people don't on the whole make decisions on a solely rational basis; decisions are made because for different people something looks good, sounds good, or feels good.

So language patterns present another opportunity to match in order to create rapport. Highly effective teachers recognize that people can have preferences for thinking in visual, auditory or kinaesthetic processes, and they can adjust their teaching approach accordingly to accommodate different learning styles. They can also take things a step further. They notice the language patterns that people use as clues to their thinking processes. By being flexible in their own language, and matching their language to others, they create rapport and enhance their communication skills.

Pause for Thought 14: Matching – stepping outside your comfort-zone

As with any new behaviour, when you first try matching it may feel awkward and unnatural – you will after all be stepping outside your usual comfort-zone. Sometimes the need to adjust your own behaviour is thrown into relief by encountering a new situation, with unfamiliar people. One of the university modules I taught required students to spend time in schools to develop their personal skills in a professional environment. It was a frequent comment from students that they found it quite a culture-shock to have to adjust their normal behaviour to relate to small children. They recognized the need to get down to their level – physically rather than figuratively – and to adjust their language and tone of voice. For some, it was quite a stretch and took some practice.

Our daughter Rachael found the same when she moved from teaching Year 6 – mostly large strapping boys as tall as she was – to a new post where she taught music across a whole primary school. She had never felt really drawn to teaching the youngest children, and felt unsure about how she would cope with moving from the top class to the youngest. Yet one day at the end of a telephone call came a delighted afterthought: 'Oh, and by the way Mum, *at last* I've got the voice for infants!'

The real point with both these examples is not how well they adjusted, but that they were *consciously aware* that in a new situation, with people very different from themselves, an adjustment to their own behaviour was needed. In both these cases the other people were children, but the principle applies whenever we encounter new people – it's just thrown into high relief when the 'other people' are very different from ourselves.

Creating rapport, step 3: Pacing and leading

Creating rapport needs to be consistent and sustained in order to maintain productive everyday working relationships with your students and colleagues. Just as the Native American adage doesn't suggest we *stand* in another person's moccasins, but rather that we need to walk some distance, for best effect, matching to create rapport needs to be a process that occurs on a regular basis. In this way, you will be pacing the other person – you'll be alongside them in their continuing experience.

While everyday working relationships will benefit if you have created rapport, where it really pays dividends is when you meet a situation where you need to influence another person; like Richard in Pause for Thought 13 or Rachael in Pause for Thought 15 you may need to influence another person to follow your lead. Some teachers who achieve positions in management think that their status alone will guarantee that people will defer to their leadership. They soon discover that, without rapport, the response from staff can be dissent, disagreement and disaffection.

When Rose was promoted to head of department in her secondary school, she was promoted over the heads of other members of staff. Being aware of the potential for resistance to her appointment, she made good use of the summer term prior to taking up the post. She took every opportunity to engage the other members of staff in conversation, asking them about their role, inviting their comments on the running of the department and finding out about their particular likes and dislikes. She worked particularly hard with one staff member who she knew had also applied for the post, and from whom she sensed an initial resistance. She knew she'd struck the right note when one day he stopped her in a corridor excitedly, 'Rose, I've just thought of something you might want to consider. What if we ...?' Rose's investment in creating rapport had paid off even before she took up her post. Pacing and leading depend for success on the quality of the rapport you have created. If the level of rapport is sufficient, the person you are working with will follow you – in your body-language, your verbal language, in your point of view.

The most satisfactory outcome for any working relationship is when decisions are reached by mutual agreement. If you hope to reach mutual agreement in any situation, matching and pacing will be essential. Agreement will be mutual because two things will be achieved:

- you will understand the other person's thinking and emotions better because you will be matching and pacing their experience, and
- the other person will be able to appreciate that you are understanding their position.

Matching and pacing are also powerful tools if another person is in a highly charged emotional state. They are effective because they allow you to demonstrate that you understand another person's experience – and once the person appreciates your understanding you will be able to lead them to a calmer state. If they have a raised voice, strong gestures, staring eyes – you can match all of these. What you *do not* match is the actual emotion; rather you are demonstrating your empathy with their feelings. Once you've established a connection, you can then change your behaviour – drop your voice, relax your body and breathing – to demonstrate a calmer state. They will be more likely to follow your lead because you have first shown you understand and appreciate their position.

At this point you may well be thinking that you've been trained to believe that the reverse is the way to deal with anger or strong emotion. Surely it's better to stay calm, talk in a soothing voice, placate the other person? But think about it. Have you ever been very angry or wound up about something, and when you've tried to tell someone, they've just remained impassive and calm, with an attitude that's saying 'There, there, don't worry'? How has that felt? My husband used to do that all the time, and I used to find it absolutely infuriating. I'd become angrier and angrier with the sheer frustration of trying to get a response from him that showed he understood how I felt.

No, if you want to lead someone to a different state – whether it's to calm them down, motivate them, help them towards a positive decision – the best place to start is where they're at. Matching and pacing will help you appreciate their position because you'll be walking in their shoes, getting inside their skin, appreciating their mental map. In that way you can gain their trust to exert a positive influence.

Pause for Thought 15: Increase the flexibility of your communication and the resistance disappears[11]

It took Rachael some years to overcome her initial nervousness and blossom into a confident professional teacher. As a newly qualified teacher in a small primary school she doubted her ability to maintain a professional demeanour towards parents in particular. In practice she discovered that most parents were friendly and supportive, and interested in their child's welfare – except one, that is. This was a mother with a particularly aggressive manner, who had had run-ins with the headteacher and her social worker, and who usually only arrived at the classroom door with some complaint or demand concerning her daughter – a troubled child called Louise. Rachael confessed that on one occasion when she had seen the mother approaching, she had hidden in the store cupboard, unable to face yet another aggressive tirade.

But as the year progressed, Rachael began to get increasingly concerned about Louise, and as Parents' Evening approached she realized she needed to raise the issue of the child's welfare with the mother. Louise was overweight, she was the only child in the class without school uniform and her clothes (and her body) were frequently unwashed, inviting ridicule from classmates. Louise had gradually become isolated, would stand alone in the playground, and more recently, when sitting at her desk, would lay her head on her arms and break into despairing weeping. Both the head and social worker had previously interviewed Louise's mother without any apparent effect on Louise's unhappy condition. But things seemed to be gradually getting worse, and Louise was increasingly unable to make progress.

'Mum, I've *got* to do something about this' was the plea down the telephone from Rachael. 'How can I get Louise's mum to realize how unhappy she is?' So we talked through a possible approach – building rapport would be crucial, matching a parental concern for Louise's welfare was important, then moving towards ways they could work together to improve Louise's situation (match – pace – lead).

It was a few days before Rachael rang again, and this time she was bursting to report how things had gone. The interview ended, Louise's mother had commented how she'd enjoyed talking to Rachael – she felt they understood each other and were able to get along. Unlike, she stressed, the interviews she'd had previously with the headteacher. And more importantly, the next day Louise had arrived at school dressed in a clean uniform, hair washed and generally spruced up.

In practical terms, there had been a problem that Louise's mother had no washing machine, and had to limit her use of the launderette due to the expense. During the interview with Rachael she agreed to find out from the social worker whether any financial help would be available.

But far more intriguing from my point of view was the fact that two experienced professionals – a headteacher and a social worker – had been unable to open up lines of communication with another adult to improve an unhappy child's condition. Yet a young woman, only at the threshold of her career, could find a basis for negotiation that could bring about positive changes to a child's life – possibly with deep and lasting effect.

Conclusion

Highly effective teachers understand that successful interpersonal relationships are vital and that creating rapport is the basis of such relationships. Not only is rapport a prerequisite of good communication, it is the essential ongoing underpinning of influence in a professional role. You cannot expect to influence, manage change and empower yourself and others if you neglect rapport as the basic building-block of relationships.

It is possible to bring into conscious awareness the process of creating rapport without distracting from the content of communication. Creating rapport may take some practice, and some relationships may prove more challenging than others, but it adds an intriguing element to personal relationships to pose the question: 'What can I try that will create rapport with this person?'

Highly effective teachers recognize the value of grounding relationships in rapport, rather than adopting a manipulative, authoritarian or domineering approach, none of which will result in professional empowerment. Rapport, of itself, can be influential in relationships, and further, creating rapport establishes a base from which to practice the behaviours of influence in the following habits.

Reflection: Creative rapport – practice is essential

Generally speaking, our focus in communicating with other people is on the *content* of the communication, rather than the *process*. We're not completely blind to all that is happening in relation to body-language communication, it's just that we usually notice this aspect at an unconscious rather than a conscious level. Making the unconscious conscious can be quite a challenge at first.

You could start by setting yourself a daily task to notice one aspect of other people's behaviour. One day you could decide to notice the different ways people use their hands when talking; another day notice how people sit or stand; on yet another, notice their facial expressions.

Start small when you decide to *match*. Pick a situation where you are in a sustained conversation with someone else so that you can observe the effect. Pick just one aspect of the other person's body-language to match. Afterwards think about how the conversation went.

Before you move to matching language, think first about your own language. Notice how your use of words reflects your own thinking preference. Then move to notice the words and phrases other people use – are they similar to your own, or do they suggest different thinking processes?

Once you make it a daily habit to match something about your colleagues' body-language or speech, you will begin to notice other things. You may find yourself having more understanding of another person's point of view. Because you are keenly observing behaviour, you will be less likely to slip into mind-reading – creating your own version of what another person is saying. You'll find yourself thinking how interesting it is to discover the detail of how people behave and speak – details you may have been unaware of previously.

Notes

1.   Senge 1990: 367.
2.   Knight 1995: 123.
3.   Gladwell 2000: 83.
4.   Laborde 1998: 196.
5.   Bandler and Grinder 1975: 14.
6.   Aronson 1972: 120.
7.   Ibid p. 16.
8.   See Gladwell 2000: 202, where he cites the work of Gordon Allport.
9.   Knight 1995: 122.
10. See Appendix I.
11. Ibid.

Habit 6: Attentive listening

People talking without speaking,
People hearing without listening[1]

Eminent psychologists have argued that ineffective listening is the greatest barrier to effective communication.[2] In my experience, skilled listening has certainly been underrated within the teaching profession. Things may have changed as teachers have become more confident in handling classroom discussion, but it's probably still the case that 'chalk and talk' is the most established teaching method, with a major element being 'teacher asks question, pupils answer, what counts as an answer is decided by teachers'.[3]

Certainly it's still a claim that the overwhelming majority of the language in the classroom comes from the teacher rather from the class.[4] Yet as the paradigm is shifting from an emphasis on didactic teaching to a focus on developing learning, the ability to demonstrate skilled listening has become even more important. Research has found that skill in listening – as well as being important for teachers' social interaction – is a vital element in pupil learning. One project used a range of cooperative tasks to help pupils foster their skills in giving information and instruction. An interesting finding was that the children who first played the role of *listener* were significantly more articulate when it came to their turn to play the role of *speaker* than the children who had first acted as speakers. The conclusion was that, provided the child had to act upon what he was told, *listening* was a more powerful vehicle for learning how to *talk* informatively than was exclusive experience as a speaker.[5]

Unfortunately, many of us will not be good role-models for skilled listening. Not just because of the dominance of teacher talk in the classroom, but because, throughout our lives, we develop improper listening habits and become expert in the art of not listening when appearing to listen, maintaining an interested expression when all the time we may be thinking about something else.[6]

Real listening is an *active* rather than a *passive* process. It is necessary to move beyond merely hearing the words spoken to noticing the nonverbal indicators of unspoken meanings. Just as rapport of itself can be influential in establishing good relationships, skilled listening can help communication flow. Moreover, it significantly contributes to the self-esteem of the people with whom you are working.

Pause for Thought 16: The starting-point for attentive listening

A starting-point for developing skilled listening is to eradicate those habits that interfere with your receptiveness. You will notice things about other people that suggest that they are hearing rather than listening to you. Some will be quite blatant, like the person in my family who turns away to occupy himself with something on the kitchen stove while protesting he's still listening to me! You will also know what it feels like to be on the receiving end of poor listening behaviour. At the very least you may find it offputting and not feel you would want to share anything of significance with that person.

One of the most dramatically effective exercises I run in training is to ask a delegate to talk for two minutes about a subject that is very dear to their heart, something they feel strongly about. Then I secretly brief a partner to listen intently for a while before they do something that will send a message they are not listening – such as breaking eye-contact, interrupting, turning away, looking at their watch. The exercise usually ends in laughter, but there's a serious purpose. There is also one consistent outcome – the flow of talk is broken and the delegate who was speaking struggles to carry on with what they were saying.

But what's *really* interesting about this exercise is the debrief when I ask the talkers how they felt when their partner stopped listening to them. These were some of the comments from a recent session:

- I was stunned.
- I felt as if what I was saying wasn't important.
- I was annoyed.
- It was like being slapped in the face.
- I felt worthless.
- I was angry.

It is amazing that these reactions were experienced in the artificial environment of training; it was not, after all, a real-life situation. Yet these strong emotions were genuinely felt. And even more amazing − *all the other person did was to stop listening.*

Read through that list again. Would you really want to activate those emotions in other people? Particularly if they are people who might be feeling vulnerable or disempowered to start with?

Far better to prepare yourself for developing skilled listening by eradicating all those subtle distractions that may be sending out 'not-listening' messages. Be aware of the signals that may be creating distance between you and another person: all the fidgeting, playing with pens, not making eye-contact, interrupting. Switch off your own self-talk and turn your whole attention to the other person. Make yourself a blank canvas in preparation for layering on the skills of attentive listening.

Listening − active rather than passive

Most social interaction involves one person listening to another, while at the same time mentally rehearsing what they are going to say − then saying it at the first chance they get!

Habit 6 is about being able to direct your whole attention to another person, adopting a more focused, attentive listening. It's about adopting a relaxed open posture that indicates you're receptive and paying attention. Not surprisingly, when people first try to listen actively, they can find the process quite tiring. It requires a concentrated effort to switch from an internal concern with your own thoughts and what you are going to say next, to focusing on what you are seeing, hearing and sensing, while at the same time checking that you are sending an appropriate message through your own body-language. In training, practising listening without any speaking for as short a time as two minutes can be quite a stretch for delegates.

You may wonder why I've included seeing and sensing in describing the active listening process. Isn't listening mainly about hearing? But it's not really surprising when you consider the elements of effective communication. Everything about a person communicates meaning to someone else. Psychologists have assessed the elements of effective communication as:

- 55 per cent posture, gestures and eye-contact
- 38 per cent voice-tone and inflection
- 7 per cent content.[7]

So if 93 per cent of communication is conveyed by nonverbal elements, we're missing a great deal if we don't actively use the full range of our senses in listening. We have, after all, two eyes and two ears and only one mouth, and that's the ratio we need to put to use in active listening.

As you developed **Habit 2** you will have become more consciously aware of the subtlety of nonverbal messages from other people. In developing your sensory acuity you will have been noticing how much more there is to notice about other people's external behaviour, and how it changes from minute to minute. You will have been learning not to make assumptions based on your own interpretation of nonverbal indicators.

And as you developed **Habit 5** you will have been able to recognize the individual language patterns that people use as indicators of their thinking processes. You will have become more attuned to clues as to whether people are thinking in pictures, thinking through sounds, processing through feelings, or mentally talking to themselves.

Adopting **Habit 6** means you will be able to build on both these skills and develop an attitude of really attentive listening. An attitude that will enable you to be alert to unspoken messages from other people. An attitude that, in helping you to be more understanding of other people's points of view, will improve your communication generally. Even further than that, as Pause for Thought 17 demonstrates, listening can be a tool for empowerment.

Pause for Thought 17: Listening in action

I've always experienced travelling by public transport as a benefit. I look upon it as a gain to have a slot of time in a day when I
can choose to read, write notes or just reflect on an issue that
needs some thought. At one school where I worked, I regularly
travelled by bus. I liked an early start so the bus was usually fairly
empty. Except for one morning when I was joined by a colleague from school. She got on the bus at one of the regular stops
and, spotting me, took the seat opposite me. Initially I felt a tinge
of resentment. It was Monday morning, I was feeling a bit slug-
gish and was using journey to get my brain into gear. I had been
thinking through a lesson I would be delivering that morning; it
was a lesson I hadn't covered before, so I was mentally rehearsing
how I would handle it. However, my colleague looked a bit
worried, so I switched off thinking about my own concerns,
focused my attention to her, and switched into listening mode.

She was on the bus because her car was in the garage for
repair. It was so inconvenient. She was not used to managing
without a car. It was annoying because she'd been in an accident
that wasn't her fault. And the other person hadn't been insured
so she was going to lose her 'no-claims' bonus. And the garage
people weren't very helpful – she was sure they were ripping
her off. Her husband hadn't been too sympathetic – you'd
think the accident had been her fault.

Even if there had been a gap in this tale of woe, I didn't have
the energy to make much verbal contribution. But fortunately
my listening skills had become second nature and on auto-pilot I
nodded, contributed the odd 'Dear, dear', and showed my concern for her plight through my facial expressions.

We got off the bus at school and walked across the yard.
As we got to the point where we separated to head to our different departments, she turned to me and touched my arm. 'I feel *so*
much better for talking with you,' she said. And she smiled for
the first time that morning.

I smiled wryly to myself as I headed for my department, and
thought how I'd lost out on my own thinking time. On the
other hand, my colleague was starting her day in a better frame
of mind. And all I'd done was listened . . .

Listening is seeing

The research that relates 93 per cent of effective communication to body-language factors shouldn't really be a surprise. There are, after all, more channels of communication than the verbal one. You will have intuitively been able to recognize a person's feelings from their physical demeanour, from their facial expressions, or from their voice, even when the words they are using may be sending out a completely different message. Even pupils can 'suss out' a teacher as the one they can play up, or the one with whom they'll have to behave – sometimes even before the teacher says anything. And at some stage you will probably have had the experience of thinking of another person, 'Well he said that, but somehow I don't think he meant it.'

After all, body-language was the first language we learnt; before we acquired verbal language we were able to understand the broad meaning of what someone was saying to us. When I say hello to my baby grandson he smiles back at me. When I talk to him he gurgles back and we have a 'conversation'. He responds correctly to my meaning, but it will be a few more years yet before he'll be able to understand the words I say to him.

Subsequently, when we have any doubt about what people are saying to us, we tend to revert back to our first channel of understanding other people. That is unless we have become so immersed in our own thoughts and opinions, or have become so 'rationalized' in our thinking that we only 'listen' for the words that someone speaks to us. That's when we will have become blind to the myriad of indicators from people's facial expressions, voice tone, and even the way they sit or stand.

So being an effective listener means checking what we can see as well as what we can hear. It means noticing when there is a mismatch between the messages we are getting from different communication channels. It's when a person's body-language doesn't match what they are saying that they come across as 'incongruent'. And it's this that causes us to question their meaning.

There is an even more vital clue that our sense of sight can offer us. If the first main purpose of listening attentively is to gain an accurate sense of a person's meaning, the second purpose will be to identify opportunities to build rapport. You will remember that **Habit 1** involved getting used to the idea that we all have unique ways of thinking; some people have a preference for thinking in pictures, others prefer to think through sounds, others process through feelings, and yet others will predominantly be talking to themselves. Then **Habit 5** included learning to recognize these thinking comfort-zones in the language that people use, so that you would be able to match the language patterns to create rapport.

Building on these in **Habit 6** we can now add an additional clue to help us recognize how other people may be thinking. It seems that when people are talking, the direction in which their eyes move gives an indication of their unique thinking comfort-zones (see Figure 15). These 'eye-accessing cues' appear to apply to about 90 per cent of people, and are one of the most obvious external clues to how people are thinking. A word of warning though: it cannot be assumed that everyone will follow these patterns, and everyone should be treated as an individual. For instance, some left-handed people will show reverse patterns, and a very few individuals may have a different organization altogether.

Nevertheless, eye-movements can be a useful clue to a person's thinking processes, and can on occasion be a very clear indicator. I can remember a short time after I first learned about this I had a very dramatic illustration of eye-accessing cues in action. I was working in a magistrate's court, and during the course of a case, a witness was being questioned by the prosecutor. 'Tell me, Mr Jones,' queried the

V^c Visual construct

Seeing images of things never seen before or seeing things differently from before.

A^c Auditory construct

Hearing sounds never heard before.

K Kinaesthetic

Feeling emotions or physical sensations.

Looking straight ahead in a defocused manner usually indicates either visual processing or a combination of processes.

V^r Visual recall

Remembering images of things seen before.

A^r Auditory recall

Remembering sounds heard before.

A^d Auditory digital

Talking to yourself.

Figure 15   Visual recall
Source: Dilts *et al.* 1980.

prosecutor, 'how far away from the defendant were you at the time of the alleged incident?' The witness paused for a moment to think, then he said, 'Now let me see . . .' At the same time his eyes shot up to the left, as he searched for the memory. (See Figure 15.)

The coordination of language and eye-accessing cues are not always as vividly evident as in this example. As with everything else you've encountered in this book so far, it can take practice to expand your attention to notice language patterns and eye-movements as well as listening to the content of a conversation. But once you become more aware, you will be surprised at how much additional information there is available to you.

It's quite fun to try this out with friends by way of practice in noticing eye-movements. Tell them you want them to think of the answer to a question, but not to say anything. Then ask them different sorts of questions and notice what their eyes do as they think of the answer. These are some examples of questions you could use:

- What colour is your front door?   (visual recall)
- What would a blue elephant with pink spots look like?
                                          (visual construct)
- What does your telephone sound like?   (auditory recall)
- What would my voice sound like speeded up?
                                          (auditory construct)
- What is 366 divided by 6?   (auditory digital)
- What does it feel like to slip into a warm bath?
                                          (kinaesthetic)

Listening is hearing

It used to be an established joke in my family that my mother had a habit of speaking as though everyone else should know what was in her mind. For instance, she might suddenly say, 'Well, I told her, I didn't think that was right.'

Pardon me, who are you talking about? Who did you tell? What didn't you think was right? It was no use, she would come out with whatever was on her mind, and whoever was present would have the task of tracking down her meaning.

To a certain extent we do something similar ourselves. In conversation with people we know well, we tend to converse in a kind of shorthand. We don't have to be completely explicit in what we say; we don't have to fill in the gaps because we will have a knowledge 'in common' between us.

So you might hear a staffroom conversation that went something like:

'Bad morning?'
'Yeees. Usual culprits. Changed them round again. Helped a bit, but hard going doing this maths topic. How about you?'
'Not too bad. Getting there. Would have to be wet play though. Be murder this afternoon.'

If the last speaker *was* being quite explicit, and expressing their full meaning, what was said would be more like:

This morning has gone quite well. Overall my class are making good progress and I feel we are on line to achieve our set aims. It's unfortunate that it's raining today because that means the children won't be able to play outside during the lunch-break. This means they won't be able to run about and get rid of their excess energy. Consequently they are likely to be quite lively this afternoon and I may have some trouble in keeping their attention on their lesson.

But of course such detail is superfluous and unnecessary because when there's a common understanding between people the detail is unspoken.

At other times of course there may be a need to fill in the gaps. Our attentive listening may mean we pick up on what is *not* being said. In which case it would be easy to fill in the gaps with your own version of what was meant. But if you really want to establish good communication you need to check the accuracy of your understanding.

Questions are one way of checking your understanding of another person's meaning. I don't mean by this that you should become an inquisitor, checking on everything that a person is saying. Sensitive but specific questioning will do several things. It will show you're listening because the questions will follow on from what the person is saying, and not be from your own point of view. Because your questions show you are listening, they will help in developing rapport. And because your questions are specific you will gain an accurate understanding of the person's meaning that will help develop good communication.

First-level questioning is about open questions being better than closed questions. A closed question is one where the answer can only be 'yes' or 'no' unless the person chooses to tell you more. So the question 'Had a bad morning?' being a closed question could result in only a 'yes' or 'no' response, and that might be the end of that conversation.

However, closed questions can always be turned around into open questions. Thus asking 'How was your morning?' means the person will have to respond with more than a 'yes' or 'no'. It's therefore a good habit to use open questions, and the trick is to remember how to frame them. Quite simply, if you start a question with What, Why, When, How, Where or Who, it will be an open question and the person will have to respond with more than 'yes' or 'no'.

The words of Rudyard Kipling can act as a reminder, even though the phraseology may be a bit dated:

> I keep six honest serving men
> (They taught me all I knew);
> Their names are What and Why and When
> And How and Where and Who.[8]

Just one word of caution. Be careful with the use of 'Why?' as unless used sensitively it can sound rather interrogative, for instance, 'Why did you do that?' It's easy for 'Why?' to become a favourite form of question, so make a mental note not to fall into that trap. A 'Why' question can always be rephrased by using one of the other options, for example:

- What happened to make you do that?
- How did it come about that you did that?

While open questions encourage people to talk generally, *second-level questioning* is precision-questioning, and can be targeted at specific outcomes. First, there are those questions that aim to fill gaps, to identify what is not being said, such as:

- What specifically ...? (i.e., What specifically was not good about this morning?)
- How exactly ...? (i.e., How exactly was it a bad morning for you?)

Secondly, there are questions that can be used as active tools to counter negative attitudes. Negativity can be pervasive and infectious. It can only take one person with a negative attitude in the staffroom to send the spirits of everyone spinning downwards. In such cases, it is useful to have a form of question that will help reframe the person's negative attitude. So when you encounter phrases like 'I couldn't do that', 'can't', 'won't be able to', 'shouldn't', 'mustn't', you could try:

What would happen if you did?

To be able to answer this question, the person has to mentally switch to thinking about what would happen if they did the thing they think they can't , or shouldn't, do. The question shows you are listening, and goes further – it can also unblock 'stuck' thinking. You may, of course, still get a response such as 'Oh, it wouldn't make any difference,' but don't underestimate the power of planting a seed that may germinate and flower into a more positive attitude at some future time. It may indeed be that the world wouldn't fall apart if they took the action they are currently unable to contemplate, and your question may move them towards realizing that.

Then there is a question that can be really useful in responding to an expression of low self-esteem in relation to achievement. Expressions such as the one I frequently encounter from students:

'I've never been any good at exams.'

To which a useful response can be:

'Never? Never ever?'

Then it's likely the conversation can continue:

'Well, I did do well at an O level once.'
'Ah – so how exactly did that happen?'
'I was really interested in the subject.'
'And what specifically did you do?'
'I worked very hard and got a good mark.'

Using precision-questioning this way can help a person shift from a negative line of thinking, and help them to identify the factors that enabled them to achieve success. It helps them to move from a 'never any good at exams' line of thinking to thinking where they can accept that they were good at an exam when they *were* interested in the subject and worked very hard.

But of course you have to be listening and aware of the expression of negativity first. Pause for Thought 17 gives you one way to have the responses readily to hand. Most important is to be alert to the 'can'ts', 'shouldn'ts' and 'won't be able tos' and see them as red flags indicating how a person's thinking processes may be limiting their behaviour in ways that may not be legitimate.[9]

Pause for Thought 18: Using your body-memory

Precision questions are so effective that it's important to have them readily to hand to put to use when needed.

Using your 'body-memory' in addition to your cognitive memory will make it doubly certain that the questions will become second nature.

What is 'body-memory'? Remember the example of touch-typing in **Habit 2** (p. 44). Extensive practice and feedback (in the form of getting it right) means that my fingers can type but I can't tell you the order of the keys on the keyboard. It's the same with any physical skill you have developed. My guess is that if I asked you to tell me how you tied shoelaces you would be unable to do so without using your hands to demonstrate. Because the memory of how to tie shoelaces is now in your physiology.

You can use your body-memory to remember anything you need. In the following way you can use it to remember the precision questions:

You are going to memorize the precision questions in your fingers. So, in readiness, lay your right hand out in front of you, palm downwards. You are going to reinforce each question by saying it out loud and at the same time tapping a particular finger.

- First (pointer) finger first – say 'What specifically . . . ?' and tap your first finger at the same time.
- Now middle finger – say 'How exactly . . . ?' and tap your middle finger at the same time.

- Next ring-finger – say 'What would happen if you did?' and tap your ring-finger at the same time.
- Finally little finger – say 'Never? Never, ever?' and tap your little finger at the same time.

Now run through the whole sequence again, saying each question and tapping each finger in turn.[10]

The questions are now in your body-memory and you have them to hand when you need them.

Listening is sensing

You will have noticed a theme throughout this book that has stressed the importance of not making judgements about other people from your own mental map. You will also now be recognizing when you're just hearing rather than attentively listening. When you're merely hearing it's likely you will be 'making up your own mind' – in other words, interpreting your own meaning of what is being said rather than listening for the other person's meaning.

Habit 5 was about learning to 'walk in another person's moccasins' in order to create rapport. With attentive listening we can not only *see* things from different perspectives, learn to *hear* where there are gaps, but also we can *feel* things from different positions.

So the 'sensing' part of listening is being able to experience different positions as well as your own. In this, as in everything else, we have a choice of where we decide to position ourselves:

First position: This is where you are hearing what another person is saying, but thinking about it from your own position, that is, interpreting what is being said from your own mental map of the world. There will be times when you may need to be in this position – perhaps when you are involved in maintaining an important point of principle. But being inflexibly stuck in this position will mean that you run the danger of coming across as dogmatic or opinionated. Being able to adopt other positions will improve your listening, and the overall quality of your communication.

Second position: This is where you are able to consider what the person is saying from their own point of view. You can do this because you are able to step into their shoes, to 'associate into' the other person's experience. You will be matching their body-language, noting the clues to their thinking processes in their language and eye-movements, recognizing the beliefs and values that underpin what they are saying. Being able to see, hear and feel the world from another person's position is an excellent way of getting a sense of how the person is feeling, to be able to understand what motivates them from their position.

Third Position: This is where you are able to take a step back and see things from the point of view of an uninvolved observer. In this position, you are able to reflect on your relationship with another person as if you were outside, or 'disassociated', from being involved in it. You will be asking questions such as:

- How are these two people getting along?
- What's the dynamic between them?
- Are they listening attentively to each other?
- Is either of them stuck in first position?
- What needs to happen to improve their communication?
- What would be likely to happen if they listened attentively?

Being able to experience different positions in listening is an important factor as you move on to develop **Habit 7**. Part of practising the behaviours of influence is being able to acknowledge another person's point of view, while at the same time being clear about your own viewpoint. The three positions of listening will help you

- to gain a sense of the difference between your own view and that of another person;
- to appreciate another person's viewpoint even though it may be different from your own;
- to recognize ways in which you might be able to influence and improve a relationship.

Conclusion

Highly effective teachers recognize the importance of skilled listening in maintaining good communication and relationships. In developing **Habit 6** they have improved their ability to understand the stance of other people, even when it is different from their own. Because their approach to listening is active rather than passive, they are able to influence relationships in positive ways.

Time spent in attentive listening is an investment in good relationships. Practising **Habit 6** means using all your senses in listening attentively in order to be able to 'tune in' to the unique thinking-zones of other people. It means listening for gaps in what people are saying, and using precision questioning to promote understanding or to move people out of negative cycles of thinking. **Habit 6** means using listening to empower people by affirming their self-respect.

Highly effective teachers have also discovered the benefits of **Habit 6** for their teaching. Because they take more time to listen, rather than just talking, they encourage their students to develop their own understanding. In practising attentive listening, they provide a role-model for students to develop their own skilled listening behaviours.

Reflection: An attitude of attentive listening

The capacity to be a skilled and understanding listener is a basic building-block of good communication. It's a capacity that is multidimensional: it creates rapport, it encourages other people to talk and it promotes self-esteem in others. It's a capacity that creates an influence base for development of the habits of assertiveness, negotiation and entrepreneurship in the coming chapters.

It's also a capacity that should not be underestimated. Using your whole self as a receptive medium, being accessible – just listening – can be the backdrop to meaningful communication. Often it can be all that is needed to empower another person. Sometimes, if you want to encourage someone to talk, you may only need to keep nodding your head. Keep nodding and they will keep talking. Try it!

Remembering that 93 per cent of communication stems from body-language factors, it's not surprising that the backdrop of attentive listening concerns what you do with your body.

Relaxed body posture	Eliminating fidgeting or distracting movements. A posture that is relaxed without slouching conveys receptiveness.

Physical openness	Turning your body to face another person. Uncrossing arms or legs so there is no physical barrier between you.
Leaning slightly forward	Indicating your involvement with what another person is saying. Being aware that you are not overdoing it and invading another person's personal space.
Making good eye-contact	Essential to be looking at another person to pick up their eye-movements and changing facial expressions. (Not the same as staring, of course, which can come across as threatening.)
Appropriate facial expressions	Relaxed facial expressions, smiling, will convey interest, but be sensitive to when smiling is not appropriate; your facial expression needs to mirror any feelings you may be picking up.
Head-nods	Head-nods show you are paying attention. Head-nods do not necessarily convey that you agree with everything another person is saying, but rather that you are attentive.[11]

Notes

1. Simon and Garfunkel, 'Sound of Silence', 1964.
2. Rogers and Roethlisberger 1952, cited in Riches 1997: 165–78.
3. Phillips 1972.
4. Fontana 1995: 88.
5. Wood 1998: 172.
6. Riches 1997: 174–5.
7. Mehrabian 1971.
8. Kipling 1902.
9. Laborde 1998: 99.
10. Adapted from ibid., pp. 95–105.
11. I have drawn on Nelson-Jones 1988. There is much more in his chapter 'Becoming a Good Listener'.

Habit 7: Practising the behaviours of influence

You've got to ac-cent-tchu-ate the positive
Elim-my-nate the negative
Latch on to the affirmative
Don't mess with Mister in-between.[1]

So far the habits have been a preparation for your role as an *empowered professional*. You've thought about your identity and how you think about your role as a teacher. You're more aware of the people you work with, and can recognize the clues that give an indication of their thinking patterns. You've made changes to avoid the build-up of negative stress. You've taken a fresh look at the way you manage your time. You can create rapport, and you've experienced the benefits of attentive listening.

If you were working in a very ordered stable world, all this would probably be enough. But in choosing teaching, you've chosen to work in a complex, challenging environment where change seems to be the only constant factor. An environment where you have to work alongside other people, and where other people's behaviour can be unpredictable, erratic or just plain difficult.

I have a little phrase that I trot out regularly during training sessions. I've said it so often that I'm now quoting myself. I express a belief that 'There's no such thing as difficult people.' It's a phrase that can elicit a range of responses from plain disbelief to hoots of derision. And I've been reminded of it on more than one occasion when I've been indulging in a moan about the irrationality of a colleague's behaviour. 'Aha,' another colleague will pounce, 'and I thought you said there was no such thing as difficult people!'

Yet it is a belief I cling to, and it's a belief that underpins **Habit 7**. There may not be difficult *people*, but people will certainly exhibit *behaviours* that are irritating, challenging or intimidating. **Habit 7** is about developing responses to deal with other people's 'difficult' behaviour. It's a habit that reminds you, when you encounter a person you find it difficult to 'get along' with, that maybe you just haven't yet been flexible enough in your own behaviour to find the key to make the working relationship harmonious and productive.

The challenging behaviour you may encounter can sometimes be pretty obvious. There will be no mistaking an aggressive parent who seems bent on an argument, and you'll know instinctively that this is a situation you have to deal with. At other times the behaviours may be more subtle, or may catch you unawares. You may not even recognize that you've been manipulated into doing something you don't really want to do, that you've been patronized, or that you've been criticized unfairly. It may be that it's only when you think about it afterwards that you begin to feel uncomfortable or resentful, or even angry that you have allowed someone to treat you in such a fashion.

What is known as assertiveness is an effective response to behaviour in other people that may seek to bully, manipulate, patronize or criticize you unfairly. It's fairly easy to list a series of assertive behaviour strategies to be put into use as needed. This is the approach that traditional training methods take – delegates will come away from a training course with a clutch of techniques and the enthusiasm to put them into practice straight away. And they may do so for a time. Until they decide the behaviour is not working for some reason, and they slip back into their old ways.

Habit 7 takes a particular approach to assertiveness that builds on the habits that have gone before. Highly effective teachers recognize that effective behaviours – whether for managing time, handling stress, or dealing assertively with 'difficult' people – are not merely about the acquisition of a set of external techniques. The techniques are just the end product; real and sustainable behaviour change emanates from changes that are made internally, by reframing attitudes, challenging limiting beliefs and clarifying beliefs and values.

That's why **Habit 7** takes an approach to assertiveness that goes beyond a set of behavioural techniques. **Habit 7** recognizes the *keys to assertiveness* that lie in the habits that have gone before, and uses these as the basis for the development of assertive behaviour.

What is assertiveness?

But before we consider the keys to assertiveness, we need to be very clear about what sort of behaviour the term 'assertiveness' refers to. In particular, I have frequently found that people can confuse assertive with aggressive behaviour. So as a starting-point, it's useful to work towards defining 'assertiveness' by thinking about what it is not.

Alison always dominates the talk in the staffroom. Her colleagues tend to tolerate her as a person with strong opinions. On the other hand, she is very dismissive of any views that differ from her own. So now nobody bothers to contradict her; disagreeing with her is seen as a waste of time. When the issue of professional development arose, even the deputy head was unable to persuade Alison to go on a particular training course to improve her teaching style. Alison claimed she had no need of any further training; there was nothing on offer that she didn't know about already. Similarly, Alison always 'sticks to her guns' and makes no concessions to the views of parents. On a number of occasions when a parent has approached her with a query about their son or daughter, the encounter has ended in disagreement. During these interviews Alison can appear quite intimidating; she frowns and raises her voice to the degree that she's almost shouting.

This is not assertiveness; Alison's behaviour is *aggressive*.

Stephen always goes along with the majority view in team-meetings. If he makes any contribution to the discussion at all, he usually speaks in such a quiet, diffident manner that nobody picks up the point he is trying to make. There are a lot of things that worry him about his teaching situation, but he would never dream of mentioning them. He would see that as complaining rather than expressing a genuine concern. At parents' evenings he tends to give a bland report on the children's progress for fear of upsetting any parents by giving constructive criticism. Stephen only ever speaks in a quiet tone of voice, he would be concerned about being accused of being bossy if he spoke in any other way. Yet he can sound apologetic, and the fact that he finds making eye-contact difficult reinforces this impression. Despite Stephen's efforts not to upset anyone, his colleagues have become increasingly irritated by his 'sitting on the fence', and tend not to include him in any meaningful discussions.

This is not assertivenes: Stephen's behaviour is *submissive*.

Patsy dislikes the idea of disagreeing with anyone openly because she fears it would lead to arguments. Nevertheless, when she disagrees with something someone has said or done, she feels a really strong need to express her views in some way. So while she may nod in agreement with the head in a staff-meeting, she's just as likely to express a totally different view when gossiping with another member of staff. Often her contribution to a discussion will be in the form of a cynical, sarcastic comment, rather than expressing an honest opinion. She often tries to express her disagreement by 'getting back' in other ways. She has been known to drag her feet when required to introduce a new way of working, to such an extent that the success of the initiative has been threatened. Then she is able to say that she knew it wouldn't work anyway. Patsy tends to stick with one ally on the staff that she can gossip with. The rest of her colleagues have become very wary of confiding in her because they know she may agree with them to their face but then go away and gossip about them.

This is not assertiveness: Patsy's behaviour is *passive aggressive*.

Aggressive, submissive and passive aggressive behaviours appear very different. Yet they all emanate from a common source. They are all exhibited by people with low self-esteem: people who have insufficient confidence in themselves to use self-assured behaviours that are congruent with their *beliefs* and *values*.

These behaviours have another factor in common. As you learned in **Habit 2**, your behaviour will influence the response of other people towards you. And as you will have noticed from the descriptions, Alison, Stephen and Patsy do not influence other people in positive, principled ways. Their behaviour may appear to work in some situations, but any advantages will be strictly short-term. Long-term, the response to these behaviours can be irritation, avoidance and lack of respect.

In contrast to these behaviours, assertiveness (see Figure 16) is about being able to communicate in direct, honest and appropriate ways, being able to stand up for your own rights while at the same time being genuinely concerned for the rights of others. It is a principled behaviour that has the best chance of earning the respect and trust of the people you work with. As described in Figure 16, it is a behaviour that grows out of acceptance of certain human rights. It can also be said that, as you have been working through the habits to this point, you have been laying the groundwork for the development of assertiveness. So we need to look for the *keys to assertiveness* now before considering specific assertiveness strategies, since you will only be able to practice the behaviours once you have discovered the key elements: the elements that make assertiveness a credible, congruent and effective choice of behaviour.

Being assertive means:

- Being open, flexible and genuinely concerned with the rights of others.
- At the same time being able to establish your own rights.
- Standing up for your own rights in such a way that you do not infringe the rights of others.
- Expressing your needs, wants, opinions, feelings and beliefs in direct, honest and appropriate ways.[2]

What are these rights?

The rights in relation to *assertiveness* are not the sort of rights that are enshrined in law. We have legal rights to protect us from discriminatory practice and to cover the conditions of our employment, such as a contract of employment, entitlement to certain working conditions, to maternity and paternity leave, to redundancy payments. You may not know the details of these legal rights, but they will be written down somewhere, and there will be people to help you (such as your union representative) if you think your legal rights are being violated.

Rather, the rights associated with assertiveness are the rights concerned with human behaviour, based around the principle of being treated as an equal human being. The concept of rights has existed for a long time. It was in 1948 that the United Nations incorporated much of the thinking in this area into the Universal Declaration of Human Rights, which sets out the rights considered necessary for human beings to lead a decent life. The rights associated with assertiveness are in line with these basic human rights.

There is no definitive list, but all books and training for assertiveness will use one form or another. The principle is that if you want to develop assertive behaviour, you first need to accept that you have a right to

- be treated with equal respect, regardless of age, race, class, sex, sexuality and disability and whether or not you are in paid work
- express your feelings and opinions (which may or may not be different from other people's)
- receive a fair hearing for your opinions and ideas
- have different needs and wishes from other people
- refuse a request without feeling guilty or selfish
- give other people honest feedback
- know of and have the opportunity to respond to criticisms made about you
- have time to think when making a decision
- be 'human' (i.e. to be wrong and make mistakes sometimes)
- say you don't understand and ask for more information
- judge if you are responsible for finding solutions to other people's problems
- not depend upon others for approval
- challenge attitudes and behaviour that put others down
- be your own self, which may be the same as, or different from, what others would like you to be.[3]

Most importantly, if you accept these as your rights, you need to accept that other people also have these rights. Therefore you will have a responsibility to ensure that other people's rights are protected as well as your own.

Figure 16   Being assertive

Keys to assertiveness

The keys to assertiveness will need to be in place before you can unlock the store-cupboard of assertive behaviour strategies. In identifying the keys we can see how the habits have been a preparation for developing assertiveness.

Beliefs and values

You have thought through the beliefs and values you hold in relation to teaching and education (**Habit 1**). You recognize that it's not enough to 'hold' beliefs – there needs to be a constant check that they are followed through in interactions with pupils and colleagues. This is also true of the assertiveness rights. Being sure about the rights, and your beliefs and values generally, gives a firm base from which to practise assertiveness by challenging inconsistencies and inequities when they occur. You will come across as congruent and trustworthy in your professional behaviour when there is a match between your behaviour and your beliefs and values.

Sensory acuity

You are no longer blinded by your own personal preoccupations but have broadened your awareness of the information available via your senses (**Habit 2**). You have become alert to the danger of prejudging or stereotyping people and situations, and can guard against it by not making assumptions about what you are seeing, hearing and sensing. Because of your raised awareness, you are more sensitive to occasions when other people resort to stereotyping or manipulative behaviours. In developing assertiveness you will build a confident foundation from which to challenge them.

Managing 'state'

You can recognize in yourself a feeling of being in control, of feeling confident, of having your mental, physical and emotional powers in alignment. And you have found a strategy for 'anchoring' that state (**Habit 2**) so that you can experience that sense of control whenever you need to act assertively.

Body awareness

Since learning that 93 per cent of communication is conveyed by non-verbal elements (**Habit 6**), you have become more aware of how other people may be perceiving you. You recognize that aggressive, submissive and passive aggressive behaviours are evident in a person's body-language: in their posture, their facial expression, their tone of voice, and the way they make eye-contact. Because you can manage your state, you can ensure your body-language conveys the right message when you want to act assertively. You stand or sit with a relaxed open posture; you keep your voice tone calm and even; you make appropriate eye-contact; you ensure that your facial expression is in line with the message you want to convey. You have learned that your body-language can carry the authority of your words, and that people are more likely to take notice of what you say if your verbal and nonverbal communication are in alignment.

Getting information

You notice that when other people are not acting assertively, their language may not be direct, and their real meanings can be hidden. Before you can respond assertively, you may need more information in order to understand their real meaning. You are able to use specific-questioning techniques (**Habit 6**) in order to check the accuracy of your understanding so that you can develop more open and honest communication.

Flexibility

You are recognizing that you can't always depend upon your meaning being perceived accurately by other people (**Habit 2**). You realize that you have to adapt your language and behaviour if you want to create rapport and get along with people. You understand that your behaviour is not who you are, and neither do you need to be stuck in one pattern of behaviour. You have shown this by being able to change your behaviour to help you take action on stress (**Habit 3**) and manage your time (**Habit 4**). Similarly, being flexible in your response to other people means you can improve communication.

Good self-esteem

How you rate yourself – your feeling of self-worth – is part of your belief system. As with all other beliefs, it will be recognized in your behaviour. Alison's boastful and domineering behaviour is really a cover for deep-seated feelings of inadequacy. Stephen's fear that people will think badly of him means he comes across as diffident and apologetic. Patsy has to bolster her feeling of self-worth by 'getting back' at people in underhand ways. Feeling good about yourself is not the same as being boastful or having an unhealthy level of self-regard. Rather it is a realistic assessment of your own worth, and – just as important – being able to accept yourself as you are. If you can't accept yourself as you are, then you won't be able to accept other people as they are. If you want to get along with other people, you first need to get along with yourself.

Responding to other people's behaviour

With the keys to assertiveness in place we can turn to some assertive-behaviour strategies. Every situation is different of course, and you need to develop the flexibility to respond appropriately. But it is a useful starting-point to have some ideas about behaviours that can be effective in certain types of situations.

Being on the receiving end of criticism, for example, may be something you find difficult to handle. It could occur if you worked with someone as self-opinionated as Alison. Suppose you had agreed to share some teaching materials with Alison, and then had forgotten to bring them in to school as arranged. Knowing Alison's style, she would be likely to be very critical, and her criticism could even extend to criticism of your overall ability. Some people might respond by accepting the criticism without questioning whether it was valid or not, or alternatively reacting with a full-blown emotional response by huffing and puffing and denying all responsibility. However, the habits have equipped you for an alternative response. Figure 17 is a guideline for adopting an assertive response to criticism.

With people like Stephen and Patsy, on the other hand, it would be unlikely that you would have to deal with criticism because of their style of not saying what they really think. When this is the case, misunderstandings can occur, and resentments can simmer unspoken. And then it's always, always the case that those resentments will surface in a far more destructive form than if they had been spoken in the first place. In Stephen's case, it may just be himself that the unspoken may harm, in contributing further to his general feeling of inadequacy. By gossiping, Patsy would be likely to stir up bad feelings amongst others that could sour the atmosphere and working relationships.

STEP 1	Listen carefully to what's being said	Value the other person's point of view
STEP 2	Avoid the emotional response	• Aggressive – denying it vehemently • Passive aggressive – sulking and saying nothing • Submissive – believing it's all true
STEP 3	Check that you understand; if not ask for more information	Use probing questions: • 'What specifically . . . ?' • 'How exactly . . . ?' • 'Never . . . never ever?'
STEP 4	Decide the truth of the criticism	Is it: • Completely true? • Partly true? • Completely untrue?
STEP 5	Respond assertively	When the criticism is *completely true*: Say so clearly: 'Yes I did forget to bring the materials.' Explain how you feel: 'I feel bad about it.' Ask how this affects others: 'Does this make things difficult for you?' When the criticism is *partly true*: Agree with the part that is true: 'You're right, I can be forgetful sometimes . . .' Deny the rest: 'But I usually have a good memory.' When the criticism is *completely untrue*: Reject the criticism firmly: 'No, I don't agree. This doesn't mean I'm stupid.' Add a positive personal statement: 'I'm an intelligent person.' Ask why they think this: 'What makes you think that?'
STEP 6	Consider what you have learnt from the criticism	Decide if you want to alter your behaviour

MOST IMPORTANT OF ALL – LET IT GO

Figure 17 Receiving criticism

An enhanced sensory acuity (**Habit 2**) will enable you to be more alert to what is being left unsaid. An ability to use specific-questioning techniques (**Habit 6**) means you will have a good chance of getting people to open up to you. From an assertive perspective you can *empower* yourself and others by creating an open and 'safe' atmosphere where people can be encouraged to express an opinion.

In expressing your opinions openly and honestly, in a manner that claims the opinions as your own – and acknowledges that they may or may not be different from anyone else's – you will be demonstrating how open and constructive debate can be established. As with all behaviours, this ability will stem from certain beliefs, which in this case are:

- I and others have the right to have opinions and for these to be different.
- I and others have the right to state opinions and to disagree.
- Disagreements do not necessarily lead to conflict.
- Opinions are not necessarily right and wrong, merely different.[4]

These beliefs can be expressed in the form of the phrasing you use, for instance in using 'I' statements to distinguish your opinion from fact:

- The way I see it is . . .
- In my experience, I've found that . . .
- As I see it . . .
- I see it rather differently . . .

Of course it is important to acknowledge other people's opinions, even if they express views that are contrary to your own. In this respect, there is a word in common usage that it's best to avoid. It's a very small word, with a very powerful negative effect. I hear it used regularly in meetings, and it's a word that can close down progress and act as a barrier to fruitful discussion.

How can a small word have such a big effect? Think about what the following phrase would sound like in a conversation:

Yes, I hear what you're saying, but . . .

The first part is acknowledging what the person is saying, but then comes that 'but'. And the effect is to cancel out the acknowledgement in order to state a different point of view. In my experience meetings can get stuck in a round of 'yes – butting' with no one prepared to give way.

As an alternative, think about how the following phrase sounds:

I can see you think that, and have you thought about it this way . . . ?

Again there's an acknowledgement of the other person's point of view. Then there's no 'but' to cancel that out. Replacing the 'but' with an 'and' makes a phrase with a very different effect; it makes it much more likely that the person will consider your point seriously because you haven't dismissed their own views with a 'but'.

Pause for Thought 19: Taking time to make a decision

It's probably a perfectly natural inclination to want to agree to a request, to go along with something a colleague may ask us to do. It can be quite difficult to say 'No' to someone we work well with – we may not want to upset them, or fear that our refusal may harm a good working relationship.

This very inclination can also mean we create difficulties for ourselves, as happened to me on occasion when I first became a trainer. Often when I had a telephone call asking if I could run a particular course on a particular date I would tend to say 'Yes' straight away. But on reflection, I would sometimes regret my quick response. I would look again at my diary and realize I might be putting myself under pressure to prepare a course within the time-frame, or maybe I wouldn't be allowing myself enough travelling time between sessions. Whatever the reason, my quick response could sometimes prove a source of stress.

So I evolved a new strategy. Whenever I got a call asking about my availability, I would first take all the details. Then I would tell the caller I needed to think about it, check a few things, and I would ring them back within the hour with a decision. I then used that time to think about all the issues and come to a decision that was right for me. Then I would ring the caller back, as promised, and give them my decision.

In our fast-paced world, we can become seduced into the idea that the ability to make a speedy decision is a trait we must acquire to be an *empowered professional*. When someone else is asking us for a decision we can become drawn into feeling that we must respond straight away. Yet by asking the question 'When do you need to know by?' you will often find that the decision doesn't need to be instant after all. And speed is not the only criterion by which to judge a decision. It's far more empowering to take the time you need to check out all the issues, and to test whether the decision 'feels right' for you. As long as you tell the other person that you will definitely be letting them know your decision within a certain time, in my experience, people are usually quite content with that arrangement. It's much more of a Win/Win situation than if you allow yourself to be rushed into a decision that doesn't turn out to be the best you could have made.

Talking yourself into assertiveness

You've seen how important beliefs are in influencing your behaviour. All our behaviour is underpinned by the beliefs that we hold, and *assertiveness* develops from a certain set of beliefs concerning human rights.

We may not think we express beliefs openly, but they can be detected in the language we use. And they are certainly evident in our self-talk. Our self-talk is the way we talk to ourselves in our heads: we mull over how we feel about things that happen to us; we mentally rehearse what we are going to say to someone; we sort through our thoughts on important issues.

Most of the time we don't notice we're engaging in self-talk. Because of this, we also don't notice how much of our self-talk is negative. Psychologists have even estimated that up to 90 per cent of self-talk can be negative. So you can see how self-talk can be the generator for a lot of 'limiting' beliefs. You can detect the influence of a limiting belief: it's when you use phrases such as 'I won't be able to . . .', 'I can't', 'I shouldn't', 'It would never happen', and so on and so forth.

So you can sense that negative self-talk could be imposing limitations on your ability to practise positive and principled behaviours. Therefore, as well as having strategies for assertive *behaviours,* we also need an assertive *thinking* strategy so we can check out our self-talk for limiting beliefs, challenge them, and reframe them into more authentic ways of thinking.

Try this approach:[5]

Step 1

First of all, think of a situation that you are going to have to deal with but are unsure how to handle. It may be something you've been putting off because you're nervous about what another person might say. Or perhaps you just don't know how to handle the situation assertively.

Step 2

Identify how you feel about this situation.

- Ask yourself, 'What am I saying to myself?'
- Think about how you're anticipating you will feel if you tackle it.
- How are you anticipating other people will react?
- Are you thinking about a worst-case scenario?

Step 3

Ask you ask yourself a series of questions to challenge negative self-talk:

- Are you exaggerating?
- Are you making assumptions?
- Are you generalizing from your previous experience?
- Could any action you've been thinking about be considered manipulative?

Step 4

Now double check with yourself:

- What are your rights in this situation?
- What are other people's rights?

Step 5

- Reframe your previous negative self-talk.
- Decide on assertive behaviour to deal with this situation.
- Decide on assertive language to use.

- Check that your feelings about the situation are now productive, i.e. if there is something that has annoyed you, check that you now feel able to deal with it assertively rather than letting resentment simmer.

Step 6
- Talk through how you intend to deal with the situation.
- Practise speaking out loud the words you intend to use.
- Check that the language is clear and direct, and stays focused on resolving the situation.
- Check that your 'state' is aligned so that your body-language is congruent with the words you use.

Then take action!

One step at a time

Of course there isn't always time to think through an appropriately assertive strategy before acting. We are often confronted by situations that demand an immediate response. And we may not always feel able to act assertively; perhaps because we don't feel ready, or we don't feel confident enough, or because the situation has caught us on the hop at a time when our mental/physical/emotional 'state' is not at it's peak.

On the other hand, you might plunge into trying to act assertively by tackling a really difficult situation first. The danger there is that, if it doesn't work out as you'd hoped, it could affect your self-confidence. It is very easy to fall back into negative self-talk and tell yourself you knew it wouldn't work, so why even bother to try?

However, a simple rule that applies to the development of any skill applies just as much to the development of assertiveness: start small and practise.

Start with small situations first that will allow you to practise the thinking processes, the language and the body state. As you grow in confidence you can move on to more difficult situations. If you don't feel you've achieved a satisfactory outcome, rather than blaming yourself, be alert to whether you have taken on board the keys to assertiveness. Assertive behaviours will develop when you have internalized the assertive rights, and you constantly check whether your language and appearance reflect your acceptance of those rights.

Conclusion

Adopting **Habit 7** and recognizing the keys to assertiveness will enable you to interact with other people in an open and flexible manner that shows genuine concern for them. At the same time you will be able to express your own views in a manner that does not disregard those of others.

Highly effective teachers recognize that behaviour can often be manipulative, patronizing or unfairly critical. They are prepared to challenge others assertively when they recognize these behaviours being used, and can resist being drawn into exhibiting those behaviours themselves. They are clear about the difference between assertiveness and aggressive and submissive behaviours. They recognize that they are not always assertive, and sometimes resort to behaviours that are not so productive. Yet they also know that by reviewing their own behaviour, they can keep developing their ability, as well as role-modelling assertive behaviour for others.

Reflection: What's your worth?

Below is the hardest exercise I ever ask delegates in training to complete. In saying that it's the hardest, I don't mean to imply that the questions are difficult. It's just that it usually needs a degree of coaxing and encouragement to get delegates to provide a response to every question. Initially there'll be some embarrassed squirming, and quite a lot of 'I can't think of anything.' In contrast, there can also on occasion be an overconfident, even boastful, response that suggests an unhealthy level of self-regard.

Your degree of self-esteem is directly linked to your ability to act assertively. Low self-esteem will lead to feeling threatened by people and situations, which results in unassertive behaviours. Boastfulness also can be a mask for insecurity and low self-esteem which results in aggressive behaviour. Being able to think realistically about your worth as a person need involve neither false modesty nor boastfulness. Rather it will be a test of your belief in yourself as a competent, well-adjusted professional.

So, write a response to each question:

- What skills are you proud to have developed?
- What is the hardest thing you have accomplished in your life?
- What do you particularly like about yourself?
- What professional ability can you recognize you've developed?
- What are you very good at?
- Which attribute have you developed that you feel good about?
- What benefit are you able bring to working with other people?

Having written down the answers, say them out loud to yourself. Make a complete sentence that you can say in a calm and confident manner, for example: 'I am proud that I have developed . . .'

Notes

1. Johnny Mercer, song. (Words by Johnny Mercer, c. 1944, Harwin Music Co. Reproduced by permission of Warner/Chappell Ltd.)
2. Open University 1992.
3. Adapted from Back and Back 1991.
4. Ibid., p. 52.
5. Ibid., p. 81.

Part III

Spreading the Influence

Habit 8: Influencing leadership behaviours

Leadership is more a state than an activity.[1]

Along with everything else in our modern world, teaching as a profession has changed radically. And for most people I speak to, there seems to be agreement on one of the aspects of change. That is, teachers in the twenty-first century can no longer consider themselves as the 'Lone Ranger'[2] of old, their main work conducted alone in their classroom. Rather, teachers now need to consider their potential as team-leaders, working with a range of other professionals such as classroom assistants, learning coaches and youth workers, in order to facilitate the learning of children and young people.

Teachers have always been leaders of course. But even their role as leaders of classes of children or young people has changed. Our increased understanding of how 'learning' works means we have moved away from dependence upon a didactic model with the teacher as 'sage on the stage'. We know that learning is more effective when the learner has more control, when the learner understands their own learning processes and the teacher acts as a 'guide on the side' in the learning process.

Just as change has impacted on the teacher's role in the classroom, changing work practices such as workforce remodelling have impacted upon the teacher's role in relation to other professionals. So it has become an important issue that teachers understand the different reality of a role that has shifted from that of an autonomous individual to that of a professional who can empower themselves and others in a multiprofessional working environment.

The habits so far have been about developing self-management and the skills of relating to other people in creating rapport, attentive listening and assertiveness. In order to apply these skills in the context of working in groups and teams, you will need to understand the factors that come into play when people work in groups. **Habit 8** therefore is about understanding the dynamics of groups, and the differences that define a group from a fully functioning and effective team. It is about applying the skills already learned to influence the work of groups and improve team functioning.

Most importantly, highly effective teachers have been able to grasp the potential of their leadership role. In adopting **Habit 8** they have recognized the difference between leadership and management, and that a leader is not always the person with the management responsibility. In fact, the person with the formal role of 'leader' may or may not possess leadership skills and be capable of leading. **Habit 8** sees 'leadership' as essentially related to a person's skills, abilities and degree of influence,[3] whatever their formal position in a group, and advocates these as essential attributes for a skilled professional.

Working in groups

The reality of your working life as a teacher will be that you constantly interact with groups of other people. You may often wish you could 'get away from it all' and find some solitary space for yourself, but for most of us who chose teaching, it's likely that our overriding preference has been to work with people rather than 'things'.

And of course, it is a part of our human state that we have a predilection for living and working in groups. One thing that we share in our common ancestry with chimpanzees and gorillas is that early in our evolution we discovered the advantages of group-living. Group-living in fact is claimed to be one of the factors that set the stage for the evolution of our vastly superior human intelligence. There's only so much brain power needed to subdue a plant or a rock, but once you start living with others it creates a pressure to maintain your position by becoming smarter. You start having to think about what others are thinking, and thinking about what others think you are thinking in order to stay one step ahead. As Stephen Pinker puts it, as far as brain power goes, there's no end to keeping up with the Joneses.[4]

The argument follows that as our brains evolved, they got bigger in order to handle the complexities of larger social groups. If you belong to a group of five people you have to understand the dynamics of the group, know how each person relates to each other, understand the different personalities and what's needed to keep each of them happy. Even a relatively small increase in the size of the group creates a significant additional social and intellectual burden. As humans, we socialize in the largest groups of all primates because we are the only ones with brains large enough to handle the complexities of such social arrangements.[5]

It's not surprising then, that 'leadership' in a group context appears to be a complex attribute. It is also somewhat indefinable in that there does not appear to be a consensus on what makes a leader as against a manager – and yet at the same time, it is something that we all recognize when we see it. However, it is an attribute that through our evolution we have developed the brain capacity to deal with. But before we can begin to identify how leadership can be defined for our purposes, we need first to understand what happens when people are in groups; how group behaviour may be different from dealing with someone one-to-one. Most importantly of course we need to understand what makes the difference between a group and a fully functioning team.

Pause for Thought 20: Your group profile

A useful starting-point in thinking about your behaviour in a group/team context is to consider the groups of which you are currently a member.

First make a list of all of them. They may range from family groups, friendship groups and sports groups to more formal teams in your work-setting. Think about whether each is a group or a team, and what makes the difference.

Alongside each, use a word to describe the *role* you think you play in this group.

Now think a bit more about your *behaviour* in each of the groups. Try to describe it honestly. Does your behaviour differ according to which group you are with? If so, how does it differ? Is there a behaviour you currently use in one group but not in another? For instance, do you find you can be assertive in one group but not in another? What might be the likely outcome if you changed your behaviour in any of the groups? How would a change of behaviour influence the function of the group or team?

Type of group/team	....
Your role	....
Your current behaviour	....
How would a change of behaviour influence the group/team?	....

Group process

Many years ago I taught in an adult education college. The courses ran for ten weeks, and in my inexperience I would plunge into teaching in the first week, anxious to ensure that I covered all the content. I frequently felt frustrated at having to go back over material when new students joined the course, and couldn't understand why the students didn't seem to gel as a group from the first week.

I suppose at that time I thought that a group or class came ready-made, and that all I needed to concentrate on was delivery of the content of the course. I had no awareness of a need to take account of group dynamics, or that different things could be happening that would affect the 'climate' in the group.

It was only some years later that I understood that groups could pass through various stages of development on their way to becoming productive teams (see Figure 18). I can remember how illuminating it was for me when I first learned about this. Everything seemed to fall into place. I could recognize that when some choppy seas were encountered around weeks 2 or 3 of a course, that was part of the *storming* stage of the group. I learned that, as long as I could keep a steady hand on the helm, I could sail the group through to the calmer waters of the *performing* stage.

Unlike a formal course, groups don't always have a specific start and finish time where the stages may be sequential. When they have, it's comparatively easy to recognize which stage they are at, and make adjustments to leadership style accordingly. In other situations individuals may join and leave groups and then the group may pass backwards and forwards through the stages. But as each stage has its own characteristics in relation to the behaviour of the members, it's useful to think about which of the stages your own group/team may be at currently, in order to identify appropriate leadership behaviour.

A useful way of understanding the group process is to think of groups as passing through stages as they move towards becoming fully functioning teams. Sometimes the stages are sequential, but this is not always the case. Some groups pass backwards and forwards as individuals join or leave. Each stage can be recognized by the behaviour of the members, and the 'climate' in the group. Consequently, each stage requires a different leadership behaviour.

Leadership of teams therefore demands not only interpersonal skills of a high order, confidence, stamina and a sense of humour, but also a strategic appreciation of the stage of development of the team.

A leader will need to appreciate that as the group matures into a team, so their leadership style needs to move on to accommodate the evolving process.

Stage 1: Forming

Climate	*Process*
Generally anxious	Poor listening skills
Polite distrust of each other or the task	Attempts to impose a structure
	Dependence on a leader or strong members
Reluctance to speak out or share feelings	Trying to get the leader to act like a 'real' leader
	Non-participation or hesitant participation by some members

Stage 2: Storming

Climate	*Process*
Tension	Negative feelings about the task or other members
Defensiveness	Questioning of the value of the task
Dragging feet, little evidence of risk-taking	Challenges to the leader
	Uneven participation (some people very involved, others withdrawn)

Stage 3: Norming

Climate	Process
More cooperation	Feelings and opinions expressed in an open and constructive way
Emergence of a sense of group identity	
Members may begin to feel affection for each other	Members dealing with each other directly by asking questions and giving support
	Acceptance of the leadership style

Stage 4: Performing

Climate	Process
Openness	Contribution from all members high and encouraged
High morale	
Safety and confidence	
Lots of energy	Group working hard at achievement of the task
Feeling of intimacy	Leader as participative member

Figure 18   The group process
Source: Based on Tuckman 1965.

Group climate

You will notice from Figure 18 that the group climate is very much associated with the emotional state of group members. Indeed, the social climate of a group can affect emotions just as much as the climate we experience outdoors. A dark, rainy day may dampen our spirits, and it can seem easier to be cheerful on a sunny day. In just the same way, the overall climate in a group can influence individual feelings.

An absolutely indispensable element of leadership is the ability to sense the climate in a group or team. Without this social awareness it is difficult to see how a leader can demonstrate empathy in responding to the feelings of group members. By being attuned to how others feel, a leader can match their own behaviour appropriately − whether it is to calm fears, soothe anger or initiate good spirits.[6]

The habits so far will have equipped you with the essential attributes to influence emotional climate. You will have developed sensory acuity so that you notice more about people's general demeanour – you will be able to pick up clues to how they are feeling. You can create rapport and will be able to use this to draw someone into a group when you sense they are being sidelined. Attentive listening is always a good attribute to ensure everyone in a group feels they are valued. You can use specific questions to sound out feelings and encourage people to air feelings that may be being left unsaid. Being assertive in a group situation means you will be able to express your own thoughts and feelings openly while at the same time taking account of other people's opinions and feelings.

Perhaps overriding all these skills is the ability to manage your emotional state (see **Habit 2**). You cannot expect to demonstrate positive leadership and influence the climate of a group if you are first not able to understand and take control of your own feelings. A strong sense of self-awareness means you can be realistic – neither too self-critical nor naïvely hopeful. When you are honest with yourself about yourself you will be able to be honest about yourself to others, even to the point of being able to laugh at your own idiosyncrasies.[7] Whatever your formal 'position' in a group, self-awareness and emotional state-management are attributes that mean you will be able to influence positively the climate of the group. As Daniel Goleman puts it, ultimately the most meaningful act of responsibility that leaders can do is to control their own state of mind.[8]

Pause for Thought 21: Sharing laughter

The sound of laughter is an indicator of a group's emotional temperature, a signal that people's hearts as well as their minds are engaged. All emotions spread like viruses, and laughter is an indicator of the contagious nature of good feelings. It's also been found that good moods such as cheerfulness and warmth spread most easily, with irritability being less contagious and depression spreading hardly at all.

Laughter has little to do with people's ability to tell a joke; it almost always comes in response to a friendly, relaxed social interaction. Smiles are the most contagious of all signals – smiles almost irresistibly attract smiles in return. In neurological terms, shared laughter is the most direct communication possible between people – an immediate involuntary reaction that links hearts before minds.[9]

Given the powerful effect of laughter on the climate of a group, it's useful to consider how often you make links with other people by means of smiles and laughter:

	Daily	Weekly	Can't remember the last time I did this
Smiled and said 'Good morning' to *everyone* in the staffroom			
Initiated laughter at a meeting to lighten the atmosphere			
Went out of your way to make a colleague smile when you thought they needed cheering up			
Set yourself up for people to laugh at you to encourage bonding in a group			
Promoted shared laughter in the staffroom			
Ensured the school day ended on a good note by leaving colleagues with a warm and loving phrase			

Of course, all the above applies to your relationship with pupils also. What would your responses be if you thought about the items in relation to your class?

Team focus

One of the main differences that defines a group from a team is that while a group may be a collection of individuals, a team will have some sort of common purpose that joins them together. However, being given a job of work to do is not enough to ensure that the individuals concerned will automatically forge themselves into an effective team, or even that the job will get done efficiently. In thinking about the teams of which you are a member, you may have been able to recognize that there are some that are loosely connected groups of individuals, while others have more of the ethos and culture of a team.

You may also have experienced that people who hold the formal roles as leaders may have different leadership styles. Some may be clearly task-orientated, keenly focused on getting the job done. They may see the main function of leadership as identifying the outcome to be achieved and allocating tasks to achieve it. Others may appear to you to be more people-orientated, possibly wanting to be 'one of the gang' rather than leading from the front. Perhaps you have found that working in one team is overall a better experience than working in another, and you may be able to relate this to feeling more motivated by a particular leadership style.

John Adair has argued that for a group to be a successful team there are certain types of need which must be met by a leader. In what he calls *action-centred leadership*.[10]

- There are the needs of the *task*. A team needs a worthwhile goal. A leader needs to ensure the goal is clear to team-members, and that there is agreement about the goal to be achieved. There needs to be a plan of action to achieve the goal, and the leader needs to help the team recognize when the goal has been achieved.
- There are *maintenance* needs of the team. The leader needs to ensure that there is common understanding between team-members and facilitate cooperation. The team needs to have an ethos of members supporting each other, even when they disagree.
- There will be *individual* needs in the team. Different team-members will have their own individual needs that the leader needs to recognize. There may be a need for recognition of a particular problem, or a need to belong. Others may have a need to contribute, or for power and status.

The important skill of the leader is recognizing that the needs of the team change over time and knowing which need to attend to at any one time. I remember a team I was involved in a long time ago, where we seemed to be struggling along, not making any progress at all on the work we should have been tackling. It was really a very frustrating experience. It was only with the benefit of hindsight that I was able to recognize that the problem lay with one member of the team, and her relationship with the leader. Because her needs in the team were not being met, she had reduced the team to a stalemate position. The leader had a fairly inflexible style, and ploughed stoically on trying to get the team to work together. So we were in an intractable situation where both leader and team-member were locked into their own attitudes and behaviour. Sadly, teamwork only improved when the individual left, and the team was able to concentrate on the task in hand.

The person with the most flexibility will control the system[11]

Yes, the 'F' word again! (see **Habit 2**). I hope that by now you have recognized how flexibility in thinking and behaviour is possibly the most important key factor in becoming an empowered professional.

Flexibility is a key factor in leadership because creating an efficient working atmosphere with a willing cooperation to get a job done means adjusting one's leadership style on the twin dimensions of task and relationship behaviour.[12] There are times, such as when you may recognize that the team is at the *performing* stage, when it will be concentrating on the work to be done. Then your specific-questioning skills will be identifying the needs of the task for the team, keeping the focus on the work in hand, and checking that everyone understands what's happening and what needs to be done. At other times, on the relationship dimension, you will appreciate how the habits have prepared you to recognize and respond to the unique individuality of other people. Particularly as, in managing, it's been recognized that treating all people the same is a recipe for difficulty and disappointment. Effective managers are those who have a capacity to sense the needs of those with whom they work and adapt their style accordingly.[13]

Just being a teacher demands flexibility. A primary school teacher is estimated to make a thousand decisions a day; interactive decisions made on the spur of the moment in response to rapid readings of the situation.[14] Flexibility is essential in thinking, language and behaviour in *all* contexts, whether interacting with children or adults, individually or in groups. Of course flexibility in language and behaviour requires the capability (see Figure 2) to understand the type of behaviour to adopt in a given situation: choosing whether to adopt a behaviour that furthers the task, or one which maintains the team, or one which supports an individual in the team.

Yet when we think about leadership of teams, we can emphasize two key points in relation to flexibility. First, that leadership behaviours can be demonstrated by anyone in a team, not just the formal leader. In fact it is a definite bonus for team effectiveness if a team-member can supplement and complement a team-leader who lacks a fully developed leadership style. Second, we can identify a range of behaviours that fit with the needs of a team.[15] These concern:

Task
- checking performance towards achievement of goals
- organizing work
- identifying problems
- recognizing the stage of progress towards the goals.
- making all the above explicit so that there is a common understanding amongst team members

Maintenance
- communicating clearly so that all team members are clear about roles and responsibilities
- articulating things that may not be being said – bringing unspoken issues to the surface so they can be discussed openly
- acting as a peacemaker to ensure consensus
- acting as honest broker to establish trust

Individual
- acting as a role-model for expected behaviour
- coaching, encouraging and supporting others
- demonstrating concern for the well-being of others

Pause for Thought 22: The cost of trust

Being able to acknowledge and build on the contributions of others implies a flexibility of mind. A person who keeps their cards close to their chest and is too possessive about their own 'territory' or information, is setting limits to their own growth, and on the group's empowerment as a team. The flexibility to be open and receptive to other people's ideas inspires trust, and as you will see from the examples below, a lack of trust can have a significantly damaging effect on teamwork.

Melanie has been appointed as English coordinator in a primary school. The school had not scored well on English in its last inspection, so she has introduced a new scheme to improve teaching and attainment. Despite having the full backing of the head, she has met quite a bit of resistance from the rest of the staff. Some of the older members of staff have said they don't see the point of the change, what's wrong with the way they have always taught English? Other less-experienced staff are rather uncertain about their ability to cope with the more demanding nature of the new scheme. There has been a distinct 'dragging of feet' and reluctance when Melanie has asked to monitor the work of individual classes to ensure there is coherent approach across the whole school. Melanie is quite new to the school; she quickly recognized the need to improve the teaching of English and her previous experience has convinced her of the value of this particular scheme. While she is frustrated that she doesn't seem to have gained the trust of her colleagues, she feels a need to press ahead with the scheme for the benefit of the children.

Gavin is a talented and energetic member of the history department. He has initiated several creative projects to improve the presentation of history throughout the department, and the rest of the staff team have taken up his ideas with enthusiasm. He has been told by a friend in another department that his latest idea has been mentioned at a meeting of senior staff. However, his friend also added that the head of department presented it as his own idea, making no mention of Gavin. Despite his usual open and sharing nature, Gavin feels resentful about this. He is wondering whether he should mention it to anyone to claim credit for his idea. More seriously, he feels disinclined to present any more ideas to the team and thinks he will have to keep them to himself.

Sandra has Monday mornings for her planning, preparation and assessment time. Her class is taken by Erica, a part-time teacher employed to cover while teachers at the school take their PPA time. Sandra always leaves work for Erica to cover with her class, but she is concerned that her class never seems to finish the work she has set. She is becoming increasingly suspicious that Erica spends some of the time on other things. When she has asked Erica about this, Erica has insisted that it's just that the class are slow in covering the work. Sandra knows her class very well, and has a good relationship with the children, so she knows the amount of work they are able to cover. She can't decide whether the persistent failure to complete the work is because Erica has poor teaching skills, or because Erica spends time doing other things.

Can you recognize examples of this sort of behaviour in your own experience? How do you think the teachers concerned could handle the situations? What do you think they should do?

Conclusion

Highly effective teachers have developed the social awareness that is a prerequisite for leadership. First and foremost, they have addressed self management, and are able to manage their emotional state and understand and take control of their feelings. Next, they have an appreciation of the importance of flexibility in responding to other people. Rather than dealing with people as if they were all the same, they can use their social awareness and sensory acuity to adapt their behaviour for the benefit of the team situation.

While our human condition has destined us to work socially, the behaviour of groups and teams is a multifaceted social phenomenon. That's why an understanding of what happens when groups of people are working together is crucial to the development of a flexible range of behaviours that can exert influence.

Leadership does not reside solely in the individual at the top, but in every person at every level who, in one way or another, acts as a leader to a group of followers.[16] As with other professional behaviours, leadership defies precise description. **Habit 8** takes one approach in highlighting the behaviour of leadership. There is also a difficulty in common with all other professional behaviour, in that when expertise is attained the factors that make up that expertise will go into unconscious competence (see **Habit 2** Reflection). When it is difficult for leaders to describe consciously what makes them effective, it will also be difficult for them to be aware of what is blocking their path to improvement. Taking the time to reflect on your own team situation and the effectiveness of your team's behaviour, will help you to develop effective leadership skills.

Reflection

For some people work is like carving a path through dense jungle. They work hard, they have to clear every step of the way by hacking at the dense undergrowth. Work is even harder because the constant cutting away has blunted their instruments. The jungle encroaches so fast they are afraid to stop to sharpen them, so they just keep going. There is very little light to guide their way; the tightly packed trees allow only a glimmer of pale sunlight to filter through. They are constantly alert to the danger that poisonous snakes or spiders might catch them unawares. Because their attention is totally taken up with the immediate work of getting through the undergrowth, and the dangers that threaten them, they have lost a sense of which direction they should be heading. For them, the only thing to do is keep going.

Some people in this group originally had the foresight to bring a map and compass with them. Before they set out they learned to tell the time of day by the movement of the sun and navigate by the stars. They tried to tell the other people how the map and compass could help; they even suggested climbing a tree to try to get sight of where they were headed. But the other people thought they were wasting their time. 'Save your energy for the jungle,' they cried. 'It's the only way.'

There is another group of people who approach work in a different way. They are high above the jungle, in a basket carried by a hot air balloon. They were told a balloon was too unreliable as a means of transport, but the people in it thought that at least there was no engine to break down. They admit they are affected by external pressures such as being blown off course by the wind, but they can compensate for this by adjusting the flaps in the

---

balloon. And if they begin to drop too low, they can release just the right amount of fire power to lift them back up again. So on the whole, they feel in control of their situation.

The main advantage of travelling by balloon is that the people in the basket can see the extent of the jungle below them and the direction in which they're headed. They are high enough to see that at one edge of the jungle there is deep chasm through which hurtles a foaming torrent. Far away in the other direction they can glimpse a wide prairie with the dust rising from the trampling of stampeding buffalo. Whenever they feel they are drifting too close to the dangers, they adjust the flaps on the balloon to move themselves back on course.

They have also been able to look down on the group making their way through the jungle and they can see when they are headed for danger. If they see they are nearing the chasm, they call out a warning, and when they see them moving toward the stampeding buffalo they shout for them to beware. But the group in the jungle seem to resent their interference. The people in the balloon have even offered to drop down a rope ladder so the people in the jungle could climb up and join them (it's a very large balloon). But the people in the jungle refused the offer of help. 'No, no,' they cried, 'what would happen when a tornado strikes? It's better to keep your feet on the ground.'

So the people in the jungle keep their heads down, hacking away at the encroaching vegetation. The people who joined them have forgotten about being able to use a compass and navigate by the stars. The people in the balloon manage their craft and enjoy the view. And they all carry on, each thinking their chosen path is the best one.

Notes

1. Gilles Pajou, cited in Dilts 1996: 31.
2. Reynolds 2006.
3. Dilts 1996: 3.
4. Pinker 1997: 193.
5. Gladwell 2000: 178–97. Malcolm Gladwell gives an interesting account of the work of British anthropologist Robin Dunbar who has developed a theory in which he works out the neocortex ratio of a particular

species (the size of the neocortex relative to the size of the brain) and from this equates the maximum group size of the animal. For *Homo sapiens* this equates at roughly 150, which Dunbar claims seems to represent the maximum number of individuals with whom we can have a genuinely social relationship.

6. Goleman 2002: 49.
7. Ibid., p. 40.
8. Ibid., p. 47.
9. Ibid., pp. 10–11.
10. Adair 1979: 10.
11. A presupposition of NLP. See Appendix I.
12. Dilts 1996: 4.
13. Whitaker 1997: 20.
14. Eraut 1993 cites Jackson's estimate of a thousand decisions a day. See also Jackson 1968.
15. I have drawn on Dawson's 1996 list of leadership functions.
16. Goleman 2002: xiv.

Habit 9: Extending the influence

Give me but one firm spot on which to stand, and I will move the earth.[1]

In one respect this habit takes us full circle. I started this book by outlining how the habits were concerned with the interpersonal component of professional practice (see Introduction). The habits that followed described the aspects of personal development that I believe form a solid base for the development of professional expertise. They encompass both self-management and the abilities to work effectively with others.

I also acknowledged that there are external pressures that exert themselves upon individual teachers: pressures which not only contribute to the complexity of teaching as a professional role but which can be active barriers to the development of a confident and empowered professionalism. As in England, where a focus on improving schools and raising student achievement within a restricted, measurable range of subjects, abilities or competences can pose a threat to a vision of a high moral and social purpose for teacher professionalism.[2]

Habit 9 challenges you to gain an understanding of your role as an education professional within the contexts of your local community, your local and national policy-making bodies and your professional association. It asks you to consider that your 'client' groups exist outside your classroom and school as well as inside: parents, employers, society as a whole. It advocates that your practice in your classroom and school can be informed by knowledge gained from educational, psychological and social research. In the global society in which we now live and work, we can recognize how the global has become the local.

Just as **Habit 8** started from a knowledge of the dynamics and processes of groups, **Habit 9** starts from an understanding of how *systems* work on a larger scale. And as **Habit 8** moved on to advocate productive group behaviour, **Habit 9** suggests there are attitudes and behaviours that can be developed that will empower us professionally by broadening our perspective. We need not be daunted by the complexity of our world, or fear that pressures from outside can threaten our individuality. **Habit 9** encourages us to come full circle by learning to reunite ourselves with other entities around us without losing our hard-won individuality.[3]

Essentially, **Habit 9** demands a shift of mind. It's a move away from a world where we see ourselves as the victims of decisions taken elsewhere, where problems are being caused by someone or something 'out there'. It's a shift of mindset from seeing ourselves as separate from the world to connected to the rest of the world; to discovering how we continually create our own reality, and most exciting of all, how we can change it.[4]

Systems thinking

The habits so far have implicitly been encouraging an attitude of enquiry about how our own actions affect the world in which we live and work. They have countered a belief system that thinks someone/something else is creating the problems you may be encountering. People who are steeped in such a reactive mindset can be deeply threatened by the systems perspective.[5] Rather, the attitudes that the habits have been developing will enable you to view the 'systems' perspective from a position of *empowerment*: a position that enables you to grasp the significance of the perspective and recognize the potential for influence.

So what is 'systems thinking' about?[6] We tend to use the word 'system' fairly widely; we speak of belief systems, family systems, political systems, economic systems, the complex system of the natural environment. We live, in fact, in a world of systems. We even refer to 'The education system of England and Wales' – so is systems thinking about understanding large organizations? Well, while it can help understand large systems, it's also much more than that. We can explain the education system as a number of different parts that come together and act as a single entity. Within that single entity, each of those different parts will themselves be a system – your school for instance. And your school will be made up of further systems: departments, classes, year-groups, etc. All these elements will relate to each other in different ways. We can choose to study any of these in isolation, and we can also seek to understand how they work together within the larger system.

A key factor of a system is that it maintains itself through the interaction of its parts. *All parts of a system depend upon each other; they all interact.* If you think about yourself as a system, you are made up of smaller systems such as your digestive system, your immune system, a nervous system and a circulatory system. Each will function as a system, yet if something goes wrong, or there is pressure on one system, it will affect the larger system. As you learned in **Habit 3**, stress on your nervous system can potentially affect all your other bodily systems.

Systems thinking is also about seeing cause–effect relationships as circles rather than connected by straight lines. You will remember from **Habit 2** the stress on the importance of feedback in developing self-knowledge and behavioural flexibility. If people respond positively towards us, we will know that our behaviour is fit for purpose. If, however, we encounter resistance, we will adjust our behaviour to overcome the resistance. If the adjustment to our behaviour is appropriate, then the resistance will be overcome and the behaviour of the other person will change. So we have a *feedback loop*, with one person's behaviour changing another person's, then that change looping back to affect the first person's behaviour.

But when we think about large complex systems, the feedback loop may not be so direct or instant. Cause and effect may be so separated by time and space that it may be difficult to recognize the connection. We can see that in the concern about global warming. It has taken many years of carbon emissions into the environment to reach a stage where the damage being done to the delicate balance of our planet's ecosystem is being recognized. Now that we have that feedback we are being urged to adjust our behaviour to lessen the damage.

What also happens when there is an attempt to introduce change into systems – whether large or small – is that there may be unintended *side-effects*. This is very clearly demonstrated in the policy–practice gap: where a government policy may turn out to have a very different effect from the original intention once it is put into practice. We can see an example both of the cause–effect time-lapse and an unintended side-effect in the education system in England. The 1988 Education Act introduced the most wide-ranging set of reforms initiated by any government since 1944. There followed an era of challenge for schools, with new standards, new tests, new inspections and new publication of school test scores. When the Conservative government of the time was followed by a Labour government in 1997, rather than taking a different view, the new administration sharpened the challenge, although putting into place additional support.[7] Their White Paper *Excellence in Schools* identified challenging targets to raise standards of education. Teachers were to continue to administer national tests at ages 7, 11, 14 and 16, and school performance, along with inspection reports, were to continue to be made public in the interests of accountability.[8]

If we move swiftly to 2006, we discover that there has been a particular side-effect of these long-term policies, one that many people (including myself) had been predicting for some time. Ofsted, the government inspection body for England, reports that, in relation to maths, teachers are generally 'teaching to the test' rather than enabling pupils to achieve a broad understanding of the principles of mathematics. Thus the pressure put on schools to raise standards, and the fact that the quality of schools is being judged by the attainment of pupils in national tests, has meant that pupils are being taught to pass exams. A *narrowing* of educational experience that perhaps was not originally envisaged by those responsible for the policies.

Influencing a system – exerting leverage

When we talk about organizations as systems it is important to recognize that we do not mean systems that exist outside ourselves. The systems have been created by human behaviour, and the structure is subtle because we are part of the structure. And if we are part of the structure this means that we often have the power to alter the structures within which we are operating.[9]

We see evidence all the time of how systems can change or break down suddenly. The change may seem dramatic because it can appear to be initiated by something quite small. It's like the pressure of steam that builds up in a kettle until it reaches boiling-point. It can be seen in events such as the fall of the Berlin Wall: there had been a build-up of political and economic reasons for this, but the actual event was swift and dramatic. Similarly, something small may occur that will seem like the 'last straw that breaks the camel's back', as for instance when a build up of stress may lead you to lose your temper over something quite trivial.[10]

But if there is a principle that dramatic change can be triggered by quite a small event, then there must also be a potential to initiate desirable changes with comparatively little effort. In this respect there are three factors that are important in knowing how and when we can affect the systems of which we are a part.

Firstly, there is the insight that can be gained from understanding that there is a *structural explanation* for events. Understanding that behaviour is influenced by what happens at a higher level is the only way that behaviour can be changed. In the example of 'teaching to the test' for instance, when we can recognize that this is a behaviour that has come about for reasons of structure − i.e., the influence of a wider political system − we can begin to question whether it is behaviour that fits with our own beliefs and values concerning education. Further, there is a role for an empowered professional in sharing their own insight and understanding with others. When structural explanations are clear and widely understood, they can have considerable impact.[11]

Secondly, understanding a system means you can also become aware of the behaviour that will bring about change. Systems maintain a stability even when they are not functioning well. In your school there may be disagreements between staff, misunderstandings between departments, yet the school as a whole still functions. Change may be resisted because people are stuck in old ways of doing things and old ways of thinking (see Pause for Thought 23). The price of stability is resistance to change.[12] Understanding how the system maintains its stability means you will also understand the key points of influence. As an example, who would many teachers say was the most influential person in their school? The person with whom it is essential to maintain a good relationship? The most likely answer would be the caretaker. In any work situation, making an effort to create rapport with a key-holder can eliminate unnecessary hindrances. Similarly, change can be surprisingly easy if you identify the right connections. Rather than struggling against resistance, knowing *where* to intervene means a small effort can get a huge result. This is the *principle of leverage*.[13]

Thirdly, however large or complex a organization, it will be maintained as a system by the interaction of its parts. Just as it may be important to know the part the caretaker contributes to the organization of the school, putting yourself in a position of empowerment means knowing how all the other parts interact together, how they are all interdependent. In my varying roles as a consultant, a researcher and a governor I am involved with different organizations. Yet because Wales is a small country, people who work in education in Wales find they meet up with the same people at different events. This makes it a lot easier to talk to each other and to understand how things work in the overall education system. Of course, I could choose to stay working at my computer, or within the confines of my 'home' college, in which case I wouldn't gain first-hand knowledge of the connections within the larger education system. And I would lose out on what O'Connor and McDermott identify as an interesting rule for influencing systems, particularly groups: 'the more connections you have, the more possible influence. *Networking brings influence*.'[14]

Pause for Thought 23

When I taught in secondary school, I was responsible for one of the modules in a new programme of study towards an award in health and social care. The students were a small group of sixth-formers, and they were required to achieve competences relating to interpersonal communication and personal support. When I became first involved with the module, the students and I discussed it, and thought about various ways they would be able to demonstrate the competences. We decided that, if they set themselves up as a peer support-group, they would have the opportunity to develop the necessary skills. They would need to acquire the skills of mentoring younger pupils, they would have to organize themselves as a group, and promote their service throughout the school.[15]

I was pleased with the way the students approached the project. It was a rather different style from the academic work to which they were accustomed, and they approached it with enthusiasm. Unfortunately, in that first year, their keenness to help others was not matched by everyone they encountered. The students identified the members of staff they needed to approach to establish the credibility of their project. Yet their efforts were often met with lack of interest and lack of encouragement. There was even an occasion when their earnest enthusiasm was ridiculed by a particular teacher. Needless to say, I had

---

to work quite hard to support their self-esteem and encourage their efforts.

You may find this a rather strange story. The learning potential of peer-mentoring schemes is widely recognized, and students of all ages are encouraged to develop their skills and, in doing so, assist younger pupils. But my experience was a long time ago, and it's not the end of the story.

A couple of years ago – a long time after I'd left, and rather to my surprise – I was contacted by the school and asked if I could provide a day's training for sixth-formers in peer-mentoring. Then came another request – could I do another day, as we're now keen for all sixth-formers to take part? And also could I come back next year? And could I train pupils in Year 8 who were being prepared to help new Year 7 pupils when they arrived at the school?

I couldn't help reflecting on the different experience of that first group of students in struggling to get their project accepted, and I commented wryly on this to a past colleague when I was next at the school. 'Ah,' she said with a knowing look, 'but then you were ahead of your time.'

Actually I don't think that was necessarily the case. But what certainly was true was that at the time my students encountered a resistance to change that was so entrenched that their small efforts made little difference. It wasn't just that people were being difficult, it was that the 'mental map'[16] of those involved had not adjusted to accommodate changing ideas of peer mentoring and independent learning. As these ideas became accepted, there was the leverage to make a significant change in this particular school system.

Being entrepreneurial

Having an understanding of how systems work provides a valuable insight. It empowers professionals if they can have the vision to understand the structural explanation. But of course knowledge itself is not enough. Knowledge alone can still result in people becoming stuck in limiting mental models that use structural explanations as the reason why goals cannot be achieved.

Rather, systems *thinking* also means challenging existing ways of thinking. It means having a belief that if you are *integral* to the system in which you live and work then as such you have the potential to change the system, rather than having the expectation that others need to change to make life easier for you. And, of course, as well as beliefs, it means having the skills to grasp the potential of a systemic way of thinking.

But why 'entrepreneurial'? Isn't being entrepreneurial about enterprise and starting a business? Just as words change in their meaning over time, ideas about what it is to be entrepreneurial have extended beyond commercial activity. It is now recognized that 'being entrepreneurial' is a way of thinking and behaving, and that entrepreneurial behaviour is not confined solely to starting and running a small enterprise. People can act entrepreneurially in all walks of life,[17] so we can also consider it as an aspect of the behaviour of a skilled professional.

A difficulty arises when we try to establish what makes an entrepreneur different from the average person. Despite a great deal of research, there remains no agreed definition of entrepreneurship.[18] In fact when we think about outstanding entrepreneurs in business, we can probably conclude that there is no stereotypical model. We can think of the example of Richard Branson: his diverse commercial ventures ranging from records to airlines, with accompanying high-risk activities that include high-altitude ballooning. Or we can think of Anita Roddick who has been an activist in generating new ways of doing business; The Body Shop was founded on a belief that economic success can be combined with stakeholder fulfilment and social and environmental change.[19]

Even if there is not a single clear model, it is still often contended that entrepreneurs display certain characteristics and patterns of behaviour. There's no agreement here either, whether over how many types of behaviour or what form they take.[20] Put very simply, I have always held a view that an entrepreneur is someone who can combine the perception to recognize opportunities with the ability to take advantage of them. And since I also think these are aptitudes that allow highly effective teachers to enhance and extend their influence, it's a useful exercise to look at some of the attributes associated with entrepreneurs, and consider how they map across to the habits (see Figure 19).

While there is a lack of consensus amongst researchers in defining the attributes of entrepreneurs, and there are limitations to the research, it is nevertheless useful to consider the attributes that are claimed. The list below is one example,[21] and it seems to me the attributes map fairly accurately across to my concept of empowered professionalism. Some are implicit in the habits, others, such as handling stress and seeking feedback, feature explicitly.

Most important is the author's claim that the attributes can be learned or acquired. Therefore, you may find it useful to reflect on your learning and development by ticking the boxes that apply to you at this stage of your acquisition of the habits.

	I am confident in my ability in this area	This applies to me most of the time, and I need to develop further in this area	I would benefit from giving close attention to this area
Total commitment, determination and perseverance			
Drive to achieve and grow			
Orientation to goals and opportunities			
Taking initiative and personal responsibility			
Persistence in problem-solving			
Sense of humour			
Seeking and using feedback			
Internal locus of control (belief that achievement of a goal is dependent upon myself and not others)			

	I am confident in my ability in this area	This applies to me most of the time, and I need to develop further in this area	I would benefit from giving close attention to this area
Tolerance of ambiguity, stress and uncertainty			
Calculated risk-taking and risk-sharing			
Low need for status and power			
Integrity and reliability			
Decisiveness, urgency and patience			
Dealing with failure			
Team-builder			
High energy, health and emotional stability			
Creativity and innovation			
High intelligence and conceptual ability			
Vision and capacity to inspire			

Figure 19   Being entrepreneurial

'Activist' professional identity

Habit 1 started this journey to empowerment by suggesting that identity was a good place to start thinking about yourself as a teaching professional. As the habits have moved though aspects of self-management, relationships with other individuals, to the potential of leadership of groups, it is quite possible that you have recognized *identity* as a complex and multifaceted concept. Perhaps one of the biggest impacts on identity can be the shift from thinking of ourselves as isolated individuals, to seeing ourselves as part of the world: understanding how the world influences our view of ourselves, and how we influence the outside world.

One of the overriding characteristics of teaching in the past has been its individualism: most teachers taught in a box.[22] Today we cannot stay isolated in the classroom, unconnected to the outside world. With the speed that knowledge, technology and society generally is moving, our students would quickly recognize us a dinosaurs.

Then there came the era when adopting the processes of business and the market was thought by governments to be the way forward to make schools efficient and effective organizations. As a result, the implications of budget-handling, competition between schools and accountability to parents and the public at large impacted upon the profession. A broad social and moral vision for education was edged out in favour a narrow, utilitarian, target-driven focus. Teachers were told what to teach and how to teach it, and advancement in the profession meant developing the skills of managing budgets and outcomes.

The world has moved on and we can't turn the clock back. In any event, as I said at the beginning, it would be inappropriate to return to the '*laissez-faire*' style of the 'progressive' educationalists of the 1970s.[23] Rather, the need for accountability has stirred us out of our comfortzone of the classroom to recognize the need to work in partnership with other professionals and with parents, and to be responsive to the public at large. The features of a potential new era are being highlighted in more than one source. Firstly, there is the recognition that schooling faces many challenges, now and in the future, and that teachers will need a new form of professionalism appropriate for the school of tomorrow.[24] This book has been one form of response to that call. Second, there has been a rallying cry that it is now vital that the teaching profession works in partnership with the public to become a vigorous *social movement* of acting subjects who work together to improve the quality and the professionalism of teaching.[25]

A third call suggests that the time is right for this movement to occur:

If the teaching profession wants to be the author of its own identity or professional narrative then now is possibly the time for this to occur. There is now some evidence suggesting that the market is no longer the appropriate metaphor or structure in which education policies and practices develop. Under more democratic conditions, where teacher knowledge and expertise are recognized and rewarded, an activist teacher professional identity fosters new forms of public and professional engagement by teachers themselves and the broader population. Activist teacher professional identity encourages new forms of association of teachers among themselves and with others. It promotes new work practices and more flexible ways of thinking about practice.[26]

By adopting the habits in relation to their own self-management, and being flexible in their thinking and behaviour, highly effective teachers are well placed to adopt an activist teacher professional identity. With an understanding of the big picture and the skills of being entreprenurial, they have the personal and professional confidence to adopt the attitudes of activism. Because they are not deterred by experiencing themselves as learners, they can establish a more democratic relationship with all the groups with whom they work: students, colleagues, parents, the wider community. Further, their commitment to their own development means they can be credible advocates for the profession as a whole. They do not bemoan the fact that we can no longer leave institutions to do the right thing.[27] Rather, by 'refusing to mind their own business'[28] highly effective teachers can act with purpose and passion, not because they despair but because they are hopeful and actively determined to make things better for their pupils.

Pause for Thought 24: Teacher activists

Mari found that attending an intensive Facing History and Ourselves course in New York radically changed her approach to teaching. Her aim was to learn new methods of teaching history, and experiencing the methods from the perspective of being a student made a massive impact on her understanding, not just of the subject but also of the way in which people learn. Using the methods the past became a tool for understanding the present: learning about the Holocaust for example became a lens through which features of everyday life could be re-examined.

Mari enthusiastically adopted the methods when teaching her own students, and she returned a second time for a further course in San Francisco. The experience was so enlightening that it stimulated a change in her whole attitude to teaching. Now if she is asked what she teaches, rather than responding 'history', her favoured response is that she teaches children.

Asha applied to be a magistrate because she knew her ethnic group was underrepresented in this aspect of public service. Yet there was also a much deeper reason, one which she found hard to put into words. She felt motivated to 'make a difference', and this seemed one way she could make a contribution to society. Asha found that being a magistrate opened her eyes to the lives of people who had previously been outside her experience. She gained an insight that made her more aware of how the life-situation of her pupils outside school could affect their learning. She now feels she is more patient and understanding with pupils; she feels able to empathize and is more likely to act on behalf of pupils when she recognizes that an intervention from a health or social work professional is needed.

Contact with Reggio Children made Angela realize she was part of a worldwide network of teachers committed to realizing the potential, talents and rights of young children. Angela returned from her visit to Reggio Emilia schools in Italy having seen how adults were used to invigorate the curriculum and progress learning in the early years. Great emphasis was placed on the importance of parents as experts on their child and the aim was to find ways to work together for the benefit of the children. Since returning Angela and her colleagues have started several initiatives to encourage parents into their school. Family numeracy and literacy sessions are run in collaboration with the Basic Skills Agency. Bring Your Parent days have been established to encourage children to bring their parents to school. Teachers are able to share their knowledge of how children learn in general to enable parents to broaden their understanding of their child's learning needs.

The inspiration gained from Angela's visit was not just confined to her school. As a union member, she was invited to present a workshop at a dissemination conference. In addition to featuring the initiatives being taken at Angela's school, the conference shared good practice from Sweden and New Zealand with the audience of teaching professionals. Apart from the conference and training opportunities, Angela finds her active union involvement an invaluable means of support both in her personal and professional life. Involvement in her union means she can keep abreast of policy changes across all the age ranges, giving her a broader contextual understanding than if she stayed within the boundaries of her own sector. At her branch meetings, members are encouraged to look at new policy proposals and raise questions. Most important for Angela, there is the stimulation of being with positive like-minded people who are there for the good of the children.

Carolyn applied for CPD funding from the General Teaching Council for Wales in order to join a group of teachers visiting schools in Texas. Carolyn's particular interest was the pastoral approach of teachers in the Texas schools they visited. However, there were several aspects of the environment of the schools that made a particular impression on her. Apart from the fact that the schools were much more spacious than her own school in Wales, she was struck by the amount of motivational material on display. At every stage of the school day, whether in the corridors, the sports hall or the classrooms, the students were exposed to banners and posters, pictures and displays that encouraged them in their learning and praised their achievements. Carolyn saw her school with fresh eyes when she returned. She was able to put into place immediate improvements to displays, but she has also found there have been long-term effects of her visit. She frequently enthuses about the inspiration gained from her trip to other members of staff, and thus the influence is rippling throughout the whole school.

Pam was soon to realize that the events of 9/11 had not just occurred in another part of the world: the aftermath was being experienced in her local community in Wales. In classroom discussions, Pam and her students expressed concern that members of the local Muslim community had experienced extreme abuse, and that racist taunts had become commonplace in school. They wanted to take some positive action to counteract prejudice and religious intolerance. Pam came up with the idea of a bracelet, something that would be fun to make and wear, but which would also have a symbolism that would engage the minds of young people. The Peace Mala bracelet was created as a simple representation of the world's religions living alongside each other in harmony, and with an overall message of unity, harmony and peace. The first Peace Malas were made by Pam's students, and proved so successful that they were able to receive a grant of £15,000 from the Prince's Trust Millennium Award to continue a youth project to promote peace, tolerance and respect in their local community. High-profile endorsements of the project were received from Pope John Paul II and the Dalai Lama, and the Peace Mala has been taken up as a teaching tool throughout Pam's school and neighbouring schools in Wales, as well as in London and the Shetland Isles.[29]

Conclusion

Highly effective teachers are visionaries. They see the potential of their students and have the energy and enthusiasm to help them achieve. They recognize that their students will be global citizens in the future, so they see it as their task to give them a broad educational preparation that will equip them for citizenship of a world that is becoming progressively smaller.

But they recognize they cannot work in isolation. They are able to engage constructively with parents, colleagues and other professionals to achieve their broad educational purpose. They are able to lift their perspective from the narrow confines of their school and see their role as education professionals within the contexts of their local community and their national education system – a global network of teaching professionals.

Highly effective teachers also have a vision for themselves as professionals in a global context. For them, the walls of the school are permeable. They seek to understand the pressures and influences that are exerted upon them from sources outside their school without resenting them or thinking of themselves as victims of forces beyond their control. They seek to broaden their knowledge of educational research and practice, not only to improve their own practice in the classroom but so that they can be informed contributors to a global network of education practitioners.

Reflection: On reflection

All creative processes require thought and reflection; inspiration doesn't come out of nowhere, there has to be a period of incubation to allow ideas to flourish and grow. As a gardener, I can recognize that a successful flowering and growth does not just depend upon the physical labour involved; a great deal of thought has also gone into the planning and maintenance of the garden. A garden is as complex and dynamic as life itself. Every single day is different as the garden responds to seasonal and climate changes.

I used to get impatient with my garden. I would bring home a particularly prized plant and expect it to burst into luxurious growth straight away. I've had several disappointments when plants didn't do as well as expected, and when they just died. Then I had to reassess: was the soil the wrong sort, did I not feed the plant enough, too much/not enough watering, was it in the wrong place, too much/not enough sun?

I've now learned that success in gardening lies as much about thinking about it as the physical action involved. I often spend time just looking at the planting: considering whether the balance overall would be better if I moved certain shrubs; identifying which plants need a little extra attention and feeding. Of course I've learned from other people as well. I've read what experts have to say and I've asked about the experiences of friends and colleagues who are successful gardeners.

It's much the same with our personal and professional development. Just as my garden responds to external change, we also respond to changes in our working environment. Just as a garden needs to be managed to thrive with the changes, we also need to manage ourselves to deal with change successfully. Just as gardening needs thought before action, we also need to use reflection as an essential tool for our growth and improvement.

Reflection has been integral to the habits. It's important because if we don't take the time to consider our own development, we may discover one day that our growth has been stunted. With reflection comes learning, and as teachers we need to be the lead learners among those with whom we come into contact.

Just as my garden comes full circle with the seasons, this book comes full circle to use the levels of thinking and experiencing featured in **Habit 1** as a tool for reflection. First time round, I described how the levels engaged different parts of the brain – they had a *neuro-logical* basis. With the experience of having worked through the habits, this time they may make a different sense – they may seem *logical*.[30] Just as my garden is never the same as a new season comes around, you may also find that you bring new insight and experience as you consider the levels again. This time round, I'm suggesting you start at the lower level of environment – and I have a particular reason for that.

Environment

Look afresh at the immediate environment of your teaching. Check whether it isolates you from the world, or whether the wider world is reflected in your immediate environment. Recognize that the environment for teaching is a microcosm of the wider world. Recognize also that learning takes place in all contexts, and all contexts for learning need to be reflected in the teaching environment.

Behaviour

Think about how your behaviour creates and influences the environment around you. Reflect on the responses you get from pupils, colleagues, parents. Use the responses as feedback on whether your behaviour is fit for purpose and able to achieve productive outcomes. Recognize that your behaviour is not who you are; it is something that can be changed and adapted.

Capability

Understand that behaviour is not always a reactive response to external stimuli, but is influenced by your mental perception. Have the capability to recognize that your behaviour does not have to be predetermined by past experience, but is flexible and can be adapted in response to a wide range of situations. Recognize when learning and development opportunities present themselves, and be able to take advantage of them. Take initiatives that will improve your professional expertise, and accept personal responsibility for the outcomes.

Beliefs and values

Acknowledge that the fundamental judgements you hold about yourself and the world around you underpin and direct your behaviour. Articulate your beliefs and values as a way of checking that your behaviour is in alignment. Check also that the mission of the organization in which you work is in alignment with your own beliefs and values. Draw inspiration from your beliefs and values to enable you to challenge inequities and inconsistencies. Draw motivation from your beliefs and values to enable you to be creative and innovative in the practice of your profession.

Identity

Have a clear sense of professional identity in relation to the people with whom you come into contact: students, colleagues, parents. Experience your professional identity as a part of the broad educational agenda in which you are engaged: using your professional identity to model the beliefs and values you hold about education.

Finally, the reason for starting from the lower level is because we can now also consider a further level – sometimes called the spiritual level. This involves having a sense of being part of something beyond ourselves. In relation to being an empowered professional it challenges us to think about how we can see ourselves as part of a broader educational movement. At this level we can think of having a vision and mission for our professional life that lifts our experience beyond the day-to-day routine.

What will be your vision?

And how will you go about achieving it?

Notes

1. Archimedes, in *Pappus Synagoge* Book 8, proposition 10, sect. 11.
2. Day 2000.
3. Csikszentmihalyi 1990: 239–40.
4. Senge 1990: 12–13.
5. Ibid.: 12. I also believe my notion of 'empowerment' is close to Peter Senge's 'personal mastery': 'Personal mastery is the discipline of continually clarifying and deepening our personal vision, of focusing our

energies, of developing patience, and of seeing reality objectively'
(Senge 1990: 7).

6. I have drawn widely on Joseph O'Connor and Ian McDermott's clear
   and cogent exposition of systems thinking: O'Connor and McDermott
   1997.

7. Barber 2001.

8. Although the UK education system covers England and Wales, since
   the Welsh Assembly was set up, Wales has gradually been developing a
   uniquely Welsh education system. One of the differences is that schools
   in Wales no longer administer a national standard assessment test (SAT)
   at the end of Key Stage 1 or 2, but rely on assessment by teachers.
   In addition, 'league-tables' of school results are not required to be published nationally.

9. Senge 1990: 44.

10. O'Connor and McDermott 1997: 19.

11. Senge 1990: 53.

12. O'Connor and McDermott 1997: 18.

13. Ibid., p. 21.

14. Ibid., p. 15.

15. For an account of how the project worked, see Turnbull 2004.

16. See **Habit 1**.

17. Kirby 2003: 112.

18. Anderson and Woodcock 1996: 12.

19. www.thebodyshopinternational.com

20. Kirby 2003: 108.

21. Adapted from Timmons *et al.*1985; also cited by Kirby 2003: 108.

22. Hargreaves 2000: 160.

23. Turnbull 2004.

24. Furlong, *et al.* 2006: 23.

25. Hargreaves 2000.

26. Sachs 2003: 135.

27. Saul 1995.

28. Hargreaves and Fullan 1998: 107.

29. www.peacemala.org.uk, Hughes 2004.

30. Dilts 1990, http://nlpuniversitypress.com

Conclusion

It remains a basic necessity for teachers that they need to be confident in their subject knowledge and highly skilled in the craft of teaching. But there are reasons why these aspects alone do not equate to an empowered teaching professional in the twenty-first century. As we have moved to a knowledge society, where social and technological change is now a constant factor, we have to question whether old ideas of what it was to be a teacher, and what it was to be a professional, are now relevant to our modern world. The teaching profession cannot stand apart from the wider social movement that is requiring professionalism to be refined in more democratic and principled ways.

This book has sought to identify the personal capacities for teachers to be able to demonstrate professional capability and to empower themselves and others. Underpinning its main themes has been a broad and all-encompassing theme. It relates to my own belief in a wider social and moral purpose for education: a purpose that transcends a narrow utilitarian focus on prescribed outcomes. The target-setting approach has been tried, and yet in the UK there are still too many children who are not achieving the basic standards of literacy and numeracy to enable them to live as fully functioning citizens. A more encompassing purpose would mean a recognition that teachers are not merely teaching a subject; they are enabling children and young adults to acquire the essential knowledge, skills and attitudes that will equip them to live as productive and fulfilled citizens.

If we have a personal accountability to this higher agenda we will seek out alliances with parents, professionals and policy-makers with whom we can cooperate to achieve this vision. If we forge links with our teaching colleagues, locally and globally, in the furtherance of this vision, we will further the credibility of our profession. If we can achieve congruence and control for ourselves, we will be able to empower ourselves professionally and we can empower others to join with us in realizing the ultimate potential for education and the teaching profession.

Appendix 1: Presuppositions of Neuro-linguistic Programming (NLP)

The presuppositions of NLP are a set of principles that underpin the model. They are like a belief system – not necessarily true statements, but if you believe them to be true, they are capable of making a difference to your life and behaviour.

There does not appear to be a definitive list, as there are slight variations according to whichever book you read. Below is the version used in this book.

Brain and body are part of the same cybernetic system   Habit 1

Our brain and body form a feedback loop that influence each other. Action or change in one will affect the other. For instance if we experience ourselves as confident professional people, our physical demeanour will reflect that thought. If we 'act as if' by physically conducting ourselves in a confident manner, our brain will accept the information from our physiology. The quickest way to change the way we think and feel about ourselves is to adopt the physical demeanour representative of the thoughts and feelings we aspire to.

The map is not the territory Habit 1
We construct our own internal mental
map of our external environment. Our
perception comes to us via our senses and
is passed through a series of filters that
allows us to select and sort the vast
amount of information available to us by
processes of deletion, distortion and
generalization. Since our own map is
unique to us because of the external and
internal influences on our personality, our
version of reality will be unique. Just as a
road map is a representation of the actual
road, our mental map is our personal re-
presentation of reality

If you always do what you've always Habit 2
done, you'll always get what you've
always had
If you keep thinking and behaving the
same way, you will get the same results.
It's easier to change your own thinking
and behaviour than that of another
person. So if you want a different result,
you need to change yourself.

The meaning of your behaviour is the Habit 2
response you get
Communication involves sending out
messages and receiving feedback. Our
intention in communicating may not
always be accurately perceived by another
person. If you don't get the response you
intended, it's an indication that your
intention has not been recognized.
Therefore you need to do something
differently to make your intention clearer.

There's no failure only feedback   Habit 2
It's a major mental 'reframe' to look at all
experiences in life as learning
opportunities!

Resistance in another person is a sign   Habit 5
of lack of rapport
There is no such thing as 'difficult
people' – just people with whom you
haven't yet created rapport.

Increase the flexibility of your   Habit 5
communication and the resistance
disappears
Adapting your own behaviour will
overcome resistance.

The person with the most flexibility   Habit 8
will control the system
Originates in systems thinking and
known as the 'Law of Requisite Variety'.[1]
In any system – human or otherwise –
the part that can adopt the most flexibility
will be the part that is the most effective.

Note

1. Ashby 1956.

Appendix 2: Unique thinking comfort-zone

If you scored most As, your comfort-zone is *auditory*. You prefer to process your thinking with sounds. You learn best when you can talk things over with someone or listen to what someone else has to say. You can be convinced more by what someone says to you than by what you read in a book. Because this is your own preference for learning, you probably give your class a lot of instructions verbally and expect them to listen to you. You will be aware of the way your students say things, as well as the content of what they are saying.

If you scored most Bs, your comfort-zone is *visual*. Your thinking process involves creating pictures in your mind, or using pictures to recall memories of past events. You understand things best when you can 'get the picture' in your mind's eye. You talk rather fast and, because you've got the picture in your head of what you're talking about, you may skim over the details. Your students may notice your tendency to use your hands a lot when talking; that's your way of describing the pictures in your mind. You'll probably use visual aids a great deal when teaching, and will have plenty of displays and pictures on the classroom walls.

If you scored most Cs, your comfort-zone is *kinaesthetic*. You process your thinking through bodily sensations and movements. You need to be in touch with the physical world around you. This may either be by involving yourself in taking lots of notes, or by moving around. You use your intuitive sense to check whether things are correct or incorrect. You normally talk slowly and breathe deeply. You sometimes think it takes you longer to grasp things than other people. You like to allow your students room to move and will use a lot of group activities.

You may either show a preference for one thinking comfort-zone, or your scores may be spread over all three. If you show a preference, think about whether your own thinking comfort-zone is evident in your style of teaching. Can you adapt your style to accommodate the differing styles of your students? Can you introduce more flexibility to 'hook in' learners who may have different thinking comfort-zones to your own?

Bibliography

Abbott, J. and Ryan, T. 2000 *The Unfinished Revolution*. Stafford: Network Educational Press.

Adair, J. 1979 *Action-Centred Leadership*. Aldershot: Gower.

Allport, G. and Postman, L. 1947 *The Psychology of Rumor*. New York: Henry Holt.

Anderson, A. H. and Woodcock, P. 1996 *Effective Entrepreneurship: A Skills and Activity-based Approach*. Oxford: Basil Blackwell.

Aronson, E. 1972 *The Social Animal* (6th edn). New York: W.H. Freeman.

Ashby, R.W. 1956 *An Introduction to Cybernetics*. London: Chapman and Hall.

Atkinson, L. 2000 'Trusting your own judgement (or allowing yourself to eat the pudding)', in T. Atkinson and G. Claxton, *The Intuitive Practitioner*. Buckingham: Open University Press, pp. 53–65.

Atkinson, T. 2000 'Learning to teach: intuitive skills and reasoned objectivity', in Atkinson, T. and Claxton, G. *The Intuitive Practitioner*. Buckingham: Open University Press, pp. 69–83.

Back, K. and Back, K. 1991 *Assertiveness at Work* (2nd edn). Maidenhead: McGraw-Hill.

Bandler, R. and Grinder, J. 1975 *The Structure of Magic I*. Palo Alto, CA: Science and Behaviour Books.

Barber, M. 2001 'High expectations and standards for all, no matter what: creating a world-class education service in England' in M. Fielding (ed.), *Taking Education Really Seriously: Four Years' Hard Labour*. London: RoutledgeFalmer, pp. 18–41.

Barnes, E., Griffiths, P., Ord, J. and Wells, D. 1998 *Face to Face with Distress: The Professional Use of Self in Psychosocial Care*. Oxford: Butterworth-Heinemann.

Bateson, G. 1972 *Steps to an Ecology of Mind*. St Albans: Paladin.

Birgerstam, P. 2002 'Intuition – the way to meaningful knowledge', *Studies in Higher Education* 27. 2: 431–44.

Brande, D. 1934 *Becoming a Writer*. London: Harcourt, Brace.

Brighouse, T. 2005 'Teachers: A Comprehensive Success', the Wales Education Lecture, Cardiff, 2 October 2005.

Brown, L. and Coles, A. 2000 'Complex decision-making in the classroom: the teacher as an intuitive practitioner', in T. Atkinson and G. Claxton, *The Intuitive Practitioner*. Buckingham: Open University Press, pp. 165–81.

Castells, M. 1997 *The Power of Identity*. Oxford: Basil Blackwell.

Coe, C.L., Wiener, S.G., Rosenberg, L.T. and Levine, S. 1985 'Endocrine and immune responses to separation and maternal loss in nonhuman primates', in M. Reite and T. Field (eds). *The Psychology of Attachment and Separation*. London: Academic Press, pp. 163–99.

Covey, Stephen, R. 1992 *The 7 Habits of Highly Successful People*. London: Simon and Schuster.

Csikszentmihalyi, M. 1997 *Finding Flow: The Psychology of Engagement with Everyday Life*. New York: Basic Books.

Dawson, S. 1996 *Analysing Organizations* (3rd edn). Basingstoke: Macmillan Press.

Day, C. 2000 'Effective leadership and reflective practice', *Reflective Practice* 1. 1: 113–27.

Dennett, D.C. 1991 *Consciousness Explained*. London: Penguin.

Dilts, R. 1990 *Changing Belief Systems with NLP*. Capitola, CA: Meta Publications.

—— 1996 *Visionary Leadership Skills*. Capitola, CA: Meta Publications.

Dilts, R., Grinder, J., Bandler, R. and Delozier, J. 1980 *Neurolinguistic Programming Vol. 1: The Study of the Structure of Subjective Experience*. Cupertino, CA: Meta Publications.

Ehrenberg, A. 1991 *Le Culte de la performance*. Paris: Calman-Levy.

Eraut, M. 1993 'The characterization and development of professional expertise in school management and in teaching', *Educational Management and Administration* 21. 4: 223–32.

—— 2000 'The Intuitive practitioner: a critical overview', in T. Atkinson and G. Claxton, *The Intuitive Practitioner*. Buckingham: Open University Press, pp. 255–68.

Etzioni, A. (ed.) 1969 *The Semi-professions and their Organization: Teachers, Nurses and Social Workers*. New York: Free Press.

Fielding, M. (ed) 2001 *Taking Education Really Seriously: Four Years' Hard Labour*. London: RoutledgeFalmer.

Fontana, D. 1995 *Psychology for Teachers* (3rd edn). New York: Palgrave.

Furlong, J., Hagger, H. and Butcher, C. 2006 *Review of Initial Teacher Training Provision in Wales*. Cardiff: Welsh Assembly Government.

Gladwell, M. 2000 *The Tipping Point: How Little Things Can Make a Big Difference*. London: Abacus.

Goleman, D. 2002 *The New Leaders: Emotional Intelligence at Work*. London: Little, Brown.

Goodson, I.F. 2003 *Professional Knowledge, Professional Lives: Studies in Education and Change*. Maidenhead: Open University Press.

Gorky, M. 1973 *The Lower Depths*. London: Eyre Methuen.

Greenfield, S. 1997 *The Human Brain: A Guided Tour*. London: Weidenfeld and Nicolson.

Hage, J. and Powers, C.H. 1992 *Post-Industrial Lives, Roles and Relationships in the 21st Century*. Newbury Park, CA: Sage Publications.

Hall, E.T. 1984 *The Dance of Life*. New York: Doubleday.

Hare, K. and Reynolds, L. 2004 *The Trainer's Toolkit: Bringing Brain-Friendly Learning to Life*. Carmarthen: Crown House.

Hargreaves, A. 2000 'Four ages of professionalism and professional learning', *Teachers and Teaching: History and Practice* 6. 2: 151–82.

—— 2003 *Teaching in the Knowledge Society: Education in the Age of Insecurity*. Maidenhead: Open University Press.

Hargreaves, A. and Fullan, M. 1998 *What's Worth Fighting for in Education?* Buckingham: Open University Press.

Hargreaves, A. and Goodson, I., series editors' preface to Sachs 2003, *The Activist Teaching Profession*. Buckingham: Open University Press.

Hoff, B. 1998 *The Tao of Pooh*. London: Menthuen.

Hoyle, E. and John P.D. 1995 *Professional Knowledge and Professional Practice*. London: Cassell.

Hughes, C. 2004 'Bracelet creates a global peace link', *Western Mail* 15 November.

Jackson, P.W. 1968 *Life in Classrooms*. New York: Holt, Rhinehart and Winston.

James, T. and Woodsmall, W. 1988 *Time-Line Therapy and the Basis of Personality*. Capitola, CA: Meta.

Kipling, R. 1902 'The Elephant's Child', *Just So Stories*. London: Macmillan.

Kirby, D.A. 2003 *Entrepreneurship*. Maidenhead: McGraw-Hill.

Knight, S. 1995 *NLP at Work: The Difference that makes the Difference in Business*. London: Nicolas Brealey.

Korzybski, A. 1933 *Science and Sanity* (4th edn). Lakeville, CT: International Non-Aristotelian Library Publishing.

Laborde, G.Z. 1998 *Influencing with Integrity: Management Skills for Communication and Negotiation*. Carmarthen: Crown House Book Co.

LeDoux, J. 1998 *The Emotional Brain*. London: Orion.

Lightman, A. 1993 *Einstein's Dreams*. London: Sceptre.

Macmurray, J. 1961 *Persons in Relation*. London: Faber & Faber.

McCulloch, G., Helsby, G. and Knight, P. 2000 *The Politics of Professionalism*. London: Continuum.

McGettrick, B. 2002 'Citizenship in the four nations', paper presented at Differences in Educating for UK Citizenship – conference jointly organized by Academy of Learned Societies for the Social Sciences and University of Glamorgan. Glamorgan Business Centre, 25 October.

Mehrabian, A. 1971 *Silent Messages*. Belmont, CA: Wadsworth.

Midgley, S. 2002 'Complex climate of human change', *Guardian Education*, 10 September.

Morgan, C. and Morris, G. 1999 *Good Teaching and Learning: Pupils and Teachers Speak*. Buckingham: Open University Press.

Morgan, C. and Murgatroyd, S. 1994 *Total Quality Management in the Public Sector*. Buckingham: Open University Press.

Morgan, G. 1997 *Imaginization: New Mindsets for Seeing, Organizing and Managing*. Thousand Oaks, CA: Sage.

Narrowing the Gap in the Performance of Schools Project: Phase II Primary Schools 2005 DfTE Information Document No. 048–05 Welsh Assembly Government.

Nelson-Jones, R. 1988 *Practical Counselling and Helping Skills* (2nd edn). London: Cassell.

NLP University http://nlpuniversitypress.com

O'Connor, J. and McDermott, I. 1996 *Principles of NLP*. London: HarperCollins.

——, —— 1997 *The Art of Systems Thinking: Essential Skills for Creativity and Problem-solving*. London: Thorsons.

Open University 1992 *Handling Stress: A Pack for Groupwork*. Milton Keynes: Open University Press.

Phillips, S.U. 1972 'Participant structures and communicative competence: Warm Springs children in community and classroom' in C.B. Cazden, D.H. Hynmes and V.P. John (eds), *Functions of Language in the Classroom*. New York: Teachers College Press.

Pinker, S. 1997 *How the Mind Works*. London: Penguin.

—— 2002 *The Blank Slate: The Modern Denial of Human Nature*. London: Penguin.

Reynolds, D. 2006 'Goodbye Lone Ranger, team leader's in town'. *Western Mail* 16 March.

Riches, C. 1997 'Communication in educational management', in M. Crawford, L. Kydd and C. Riches (eds), *Leadership and Teams in Educational Management*. Buckingham: Open University Press, pp. 165–78.

Rogers, C.R. and Roethlisberger, F.J. 1952 'Barriers and gateways to communication', *Harvard Business Review* 30: 44–9.

Sachs, J. 2003 *The Activist Teaching Profession*. Buckingham: Open University Press.

Saul, J. 1995 *The Unconscious Civilization*. Toronto: Anansi Press.

Senge, P. 1990 *The Fifth Discipline: The Art and Practice of the Learning Organization*. London: Century.

Sennett, R. 1998 *The Corrosion of Character: The Personal Consequences of Work in the New Capitalism*. New York: W.W. Norton.

Smith, A. 1996 *Accelerated Learning in the Classroom*. Stafford: Network Educational Press.

Solomon, R.C. and Flores, F. 2001 *Building Trust: in Business, Politics, Relationships and Life*. NY: Oxford University Press.

Stenhouse Consulting, www.stenhouseconsulting.co.uk

Timmons, J.A., Smollen, L.E. and Dingee, A.L.M. 1985 *New Venture Creation*. Homewood, IL: Irwin.

Tuckman, B.W. 1965 'Developmental sequences in small groups'. *Psychological Bulletin* 63: 384–99.

Turnbull, J. 2004 'Educating for citizenship in Wales: challenges and opportunities', *Welsh Journal of Education* 12. 2: 65–82.

Turnbull, J. and Beese, J. 2000 'Negotiating the boundaries: the experience of the mental health nurse at the interface with the criminal justice system', *Journal of Psychiatric and Mental Health Nursing* 7: 289–96.

Watson, J.B. and Rayner, R. 1920 'Conditioned emotional reactions', *Journal of Experimental Psychology* 3: 1–14.

Whitaker, P. 1997 'Changes in professional development: the personal dimension' in L. Kydd, M. Crawford and C. Riches *Professional Development for Educational Management*. Buckingham: Open University Press, pp. 11–25.

Whitty, G. 2000 'Teacher professionalism in new times', *Journal of In-Service Education* 26. 2: 281–93.

Wood, D. 1998 *How Children Think and Learn* (2nd edn). Oxford: Basil Blackwell.

Index

An 'f.' after a page number indicates the inclusion of a figure; an 'n.' indicates a note.

accountability 179
achievable goals 87, 88–9
ACORN (acting as if, checking, ownership, resources, now do it) goals 88–90
acquisition, of entrepreneurialism 177–8f.
action-centred leadership 161
active listening 118
  demands from 119–20
  scope 120–1
activist professional identity 179–83
Adair, J. 168n. 10
adaptability 27
  from matching 104–8f., 110–11
    to preferred styles 109f.
  to preferred styles 28–9, 30, 42–3
  scope 42
  see also flexibility
affinity 104 *see also* rapport
aggression
  assertiveness and 135
    and passive aggression 136
agreement 112
analytical processing, intuition and 38f., 39

anchoring 48–9, 50–1
  from stability-zones 91–3
anxiety 63
assertiveness 55
  aggression and 135
    passive 136
  building up 147
  constraints on 147
  in decision-making 144–5
  keys to 139–41
  response strategies 141–5f.
  rights in 136–8f.
  scope 134, 136–7f., 148
  self-esteem and 136, 148
  on self-talk 145–7
  submissiveness and 135–6
assessment, on environment 23
attainment, understanding and 172
auditory, kinaesthetic, visual styles 28, 29–30, 31–2, 33n. 16, 109f., 122, 123–4f., 193–4
  anchoring from 49, 50–1

Bandler, R. 123f.
Beese, J. 33n. 3
behaviour 78
  change in 173
    results on 191

as difficult 59, 133–4, 192 *see also* assertiveness
entrepreneurial 175, 176–8f.
feedback on 44–7, 171
on groups and teams 155–6
identity and 34
improving 148
as logical level 185
as neuro-logical level 23–4f., 94
see also adaptability; flexibility
beliefs
language for 143–4, 145, 146–7
as negative 145–6
as opinions 143–4
principal 23
strategies on 146–7
values and 22–5f., 59, 94–5, 139, 186
Birgerstam, P. 53n. 3
blind spots 36, 37f., 39–40, 100–1, 102f.
body
brain function and 25
feedback on 190
consciousness in 69
body language 41, 120, 122, 123–4f., 131–2
awareness, as assertiveness key 139–40
matching 104–8f.
body-memory 128–9
body time
mechanical time and 76f.
prime time 90–1
brain function 7
analytical and intuitive 38f., 39
body and 25
feedback on 190
on groups 154–5, 167–8n. 5
as learning 26

mind and 26
neuro-logical levels 23–5f., 94–5
scope 17, 25–6, 27
stimuli on 26
see also thinking
Brande, D. 53n. 9
breathing 106f.
business policies 179
'but', overuse of 143–4

capability 59
as logical level 185
as neuro-logical level 24f., 94
challenges 62–3, 67
skills and 68
'changing the lights' 62–3
choice 9–10
complexities 51
in negative and positive attitudes 59–63, 64–5
scope 63
climate 158–9
closed questions 126
comfort-zones 28–30, 31–2, 33n. 16, 41, 108–10f., 123–4f., 193–4
communication 99, 104–10f., 112–14, 192
classification of 120, 131–2
consciousness in 115–16
disparities 122
feedback on 191
listening on 117, 118–19, 131
networking 173–4
scope 122, 124–5
see also rapport
communities, person-centred 6
competence, consciousness in 52
confidence 8, 34
disparities 20–1
low 136

continuing professional
  development (CPD)   2, 3, 59
  intransigence on   174–5
control   56, 159, 166–7, 192
  from choice   59–60, 63
  of time *see* time-management
Covey, S. R.   84f., 86f., 95n.   1
CPD (continuing professional
  development)   2, 3, 59
  intransigence on   174–5
creativity   3
crisis-management   85
criticism, assertiveness on   141,
  142f.
Csikszentmihalyi, M.   67, 68–9,
  73n. 16
cultures   77

deadlines   81
decision-making, pacing in
  144–5
delaying tactics   38f., 82–3
deletion   102f.
Delozier, J.   123f.
difficult behaviour   59
  assertiveness on *see* assertiveness
  rapport and   192
  scope   133–4
difficult environments   133
Dilts, R.   123f.
discord   99
discrimination   102f.
displays   182
distance   65–7f., 166–7
distortion   102f.
Dunbar, R.   167–8n. 5

Education Act (1988)   171–2
efficiency, effectiveness and   84
Einstein, A.   23
emotions
  climate of   158–9

consciousness in   57, 69
control of   159
distance on   65–7f.
emotional intelligence   7
involvement from   20
responses from   25
writing on   63–5
empathy   112, 129–30, 158
empowerment   170, 188–9
  consciousness in   52
  see also individual terms
energy renewal   91–3
engagement   80
enjoyment   82
entrepreneurialism   175
  scope   176–8f.
environment   58
  change in   184
  as difficult   133
  expertise, relationships and   5f.
  location   107–8
  as logical level   185
  mapping   27–8, 191
  as neuro-logical level   23, 24f.,
    94
  noticing   43
esteem, self-esteem   136, 140–1,
  148–9
Excellence in Schools (White Paper)
  172
expertise
  consciousness in   44
  environment, relationships and
    5f.
  expectations on   2
expressions   132
eye-contact   132
eye-movement   123–4f.

facial expressions   132
facilitation   4, 153
failure, feedback and   192

features
  feedback on 46
  noticing 43–4f.
feedback 36, 44
  accuracy in 45, 191
  external and internal 45
  failure and 192
  loops in 171, 190
  as positive 47
  scope 47
  specificity in 46–7
  ways of asking for 45
feel-good factors 50–1
flexibility 3, 76f., 171
  from anchoring 48–9, 50–1
  as assertiveness key 140
  on communication 113–14,
    192
  constraints from 47–8
  control from 192
  expansion 34
  on information received 45
  primacy 162–3
  scope 48, 51–2, 162–3
  on trust 163–5
  see also adaptability
future challenges 3–4, 179
  past, present and 77–80

General Teaching Council for
    Wales 1
generalization 103f.
gestures 105f.
Gladwell, M. 167–8n. 5
global factors
  individuality and 169–70,
    179
  local factors and 169, 183
goals 161, 163
  ACORN test on 88–90
  ambitions on 87–90
  hollow victories 87, 88

negative and positive attitudes
    on 86
  SMART test on 87
gossiping 136
government policies 19
  constraints from 6–7, 9, 48,
    179
  side-effects 171–2
  scrutiny from 1, 172
Grinder, J. 123f.
groups 165, 167–8n. 5
  climate 158–9
  developmental stages 156–8f.
  intransigence on 174–5
  laughter and smiling in
    159–60
  profiles 155–6
  scope 154–5
  teams from see teams

head-nodding 131, 132
health 57
hearing, listening and 117–19,
    125–8, 129 see also visual,
    auditory, kinaesthetic styles
Helsby, G. 13n. 27
human rights 137–8f.

identity
  activist professional identity
    179–83
  behaviour and 34
  confidence on 20–1, 34
  disparities 17–18
  doubts on 18, 19
  investment from 20
  as logical level 186
  as neuro-logical level 24f., 25,
    95
  role and 17–18, 19–20, 21–2
  scope 178–9

illness   57
importance, urgency and   84–6f.
individuality, global factors and
    169–70, 179
inertia, assertiveness and   135–6
information
    consciousness in   100–1
    gathering, as assertiveness key
        140
    perceptions on   45, 46f.
    processing from   100–1,
        102–3f.
    specificity on   46–7
information technology   2
intelligence, emotional   7
intimidation   135
intransigence   135, 174–5
intuition
    analytical processing and   38f.,
        39
    certainty in   35
        from feedback   36, 44–7
        from sensory acuity   36–8,
            39–41, 43–4f.
    scope   35, 38–9

Johari Window   45, 46f.
journals   63–4
judgement, from intuition   35,
    36–8f., 39

kinaesthetic, auditory, visual
        styles   28, 29–30, 31–2, 33n.
        16, 109f., 122, 123–4f.,
        193–4
    anchoring from   49, 50–1
Kipling, R.   126
Knight, P.   13n.   27
Knight, S.   99
knowledge   83
    disparities   35, 175
    expansion   3, 34

expertise from   2, 5f., 44
sensory acuity as   36–8, 39–41,
    43–4f.

language   57, 77–8, 115–16 see
    also individual terms
laughter, sharing   159–60
Law of Requisite Variety   192
leadership   8–9
    action-centred   161
    on climate   158–9
    complexities   155
    facilitation on   153
    flexibility in   162, 163
    on needs-resolution   161–2
    pacing in   111–14
    scope   154, 157f., 165–6
    styles   161, 162
    trust on   164–5
leaning forwards   132
learning   7, 26
    of entrepreneurialism
        177–8f.
    from feedback   36, 44–7
    listening on   117
    ownership in   153
learning curves   18
legal rights   137f.
letters   64–5
levels
    of logic   185–6
    of questions   126–9
    of rapport   101
    of thinking   94–5
        differentiation from   23
        hierarchy from   23–5f.
Lightman, A.   76
limbic system   24–5
listening
    active   118, 119–21
    constraints on   117
    disparities on   121

empathy on   129–30
hearing and   117–19, 125–8,
   129 *see also* visual, auditory,
   kinaesthetic styles
on learning   117
other people on   129–30
questions in   125–9
scope   130–2
shorthand from   124–5
vision in   122, 123–4f.
local factors, global factors and
   169, 183
location   107–8
logic, levels of   185–6
Luft, J.   46f.

McCulloch, G.   13n. 27
McDermott, I.   174
management posts, choice on
   59–62
mapping
behaviour from   78
bridging   101
delineation in   27
on goals   88–90
linear   77–8
on listening   129–30
past, present and future from
   77–9
   engagement on   80
   time-management from   80
personalized   27–8, 191
   constraints from   39–40
'in time' and 'through time'
   78–81
market policies   179
matching
from language   104–11f.,
   115–16
from leadership and pacing
   111–14
measurable goals   87

mechanical time, body time and
   76f.
metacognition   17, 27
levels of thinking   23–5f.,
   94–5
mind, brain function and   26
moral and social education   188
motivation
from challenges   62–3, 67
materials for   182
negative and positive   60–1
movements   105f., 107
multi-skilling   34
music   49

needs-resolution   161–2
networking   173–4
neurolinguistic programming
   (NLP), presuppositions
   190–2
noticing   100–1, 102f.
scope   39–40, 43–4f., 115–16

O'Connor, J.   174
open questions   126
openness   132
opinions   143–4
ownership   153
of goals   89

pacing
in decision-making   144–5
in leadership   111–14
parents   181
partnership, public   179–80, 183,
   188–9 *see also* relationships;
   teams
passive aggression   136
paths of work, distance on   166–7
Pavlov, I. P.   49
peer-mentoring, intransigence on
   174–5

performance
  consciousness in   44
  personal skills and   5–6
  scrutinized   1
person-centred communities   6
personal mastery   186–7n.   5
personal skills   5–6 *see also*
    individual terms
personal states
  management of   48–9
    as assertiveness keys   139
  stimuli on   49–51
photographs   49
physiology
  body-memory   128–9
  change in   25
  movements   105f., 107
  as well-being   69
  see also body language; brain
    function
posture   105f., 131
precision-questions   126–9
prescriptive measures   1, 6–7, 9,
    169, 179, 188
  side-effects   171–2
prime time   90–1
procrastination
  constraints from   81
  distraction activities   81
  game plan   82–3
professionalism
  activist professional identity
    179–83
  change in   2, 153, 184
  complexities   3–4
  constraints on   169
  expectations on   2
  as indefinable   2
  new   3–4, 9, 179, 188
  from representation   1
  scope   169
  scrutinized   1–2

status and   1, 2
  see also individual terms
public partnership   179–80, 183,
    188–9 *see also* relationships;
    teams
public scrutiny   1–2, 172, 179

quality of service   4–5f.
questions
  levels of   126–9
  scope   125

rapport   8
  difficult behaviour and   192
  from language   104–11f.,
    115–16
  from leading and pacing
    111–14
  levels of   101
  primacy   101, 103–4
  scope   99–100, 101, 115
  see also communication
realistic goals   87, 88–9
reflection
  on behaviour   45
  on comfort-zones   31–2
  on empowerment   52
  on levels of logic   185–6
  on listening   131–2
  on prioritization   10–12
  on rapport   115–16
  on reflection   184
  on relaxation   70–2
  on time-management   94–5
  on work paths   166–7
  on worth   148–9
Reggio Emilia systems   181
relationships   8, 45, 99, 100, 101,
    107–8
  agreement on   112
  environment, expertise and   5f.
  functional and personal   5–6

other people on 110–11
scope 115
see also public partnership; teams
relaxation 70–2
religious tolerance 182–3
resentment 141
resources 182
for goals 90
rights
legal and human 137–8f.
scope 136–7
roles
change in 153
confidence on 20–1
doubts on 18–19, 20
identity and 17–18, 19–20,
21–2
management as 59–62
see also leadership

Sachs, J. 187n. 26
self-esteem 149
assertiveness and 136, 148
as assertiveness key 140–1
self-talk
as negative 145–6
strategies on 146–7
self-worth 148–9
Senge, P. 186–7n. 5
Sennett, R. 47–8
senses
assessment from 23
thinking from 27, 28, 29–30,
31–2, 33n. 16, 193–4
sensory acuity 8, 158–9
as assertiveness key 139
consciousness in 36–7, 38
definitions 39
from delaying tactics 38f.
information processing from
100–1, 102–3f.
from language 40–1

on listening 120
from noticing 39–40, 43–4f.
rapport from 104–14f.
selection in 36–8
sensory-grounded language
40–1
shorthand, understanding from
124–5
sleep, writing for 64
SMART (specific, measurable,
achievable, realistic,
time-related) goals 87
smiling 160
social and moral education 188
society
activist professional identity
179–83
change in 3–4
stability 173
stability-zones 91–3
stress 8, 80
from behaviour 59
from beliefs and values 59
from capability 59
choice on 64–5
control on 56
definitions 54
distance on 65–7f.
emotional responses 57, 63–7,
69
from environment 58
fight-or-flight responses 56–7
as flow 68–9
growth in 54
health implications 57
other people on 55
writing on 64–5
on physiology 69
as positive 67–9
from procrastination 81
range of strategies on 57–8f.,
70

stress (*continued*)
  scrutinized   54
  thinking on   59–63, 69
  time-management on *see*
    time-management
  unidentified stressors   58
  as unsolvable   65, 67
  from work-life   55
submissiveness, assertiveness and
  135–6
systems thinking
  cause-effect in   171
  change in
    entrepreneurial   176–8f.
    principle of leverage   173
    small effort   173
    small leverage   172–3
    structural explanations   173
  constraints on   171–2
  interaction in   171
  knowledge in   175
  networking in   173–4
  scope   170–1

talk, self-talk   145–7
teams   165
  developmental stages   156–8f.,
    162
  goals   161, 163
  groups and   153–4, 160–1
  individual needs in   161, 163
  maintenance needs in   161, 163
  needs-resolution in   161–2
  profiles   155–6
  rapport on   103–4
  see also public partnership;
    relationships
thinking   7–8
  assertiveness on   145–7
  change in, results on   191
  consciousness in   69

eye-movement in   123–4f.
identity and role   17–22
information processing from
  101, 102–3f.
levels of   23–5f., 94–5
metacognition   17, 23–5f., 27,
  94–5
negative and positive   59–63
personalized   28–30, 31–2,
  33n. 16, 122–3, 193–4
primacy   17
scope   30–1
systems thinking   170–4,
  175–8f.
understanding from   27–8
see also brain function
time
  artificial use of   74
  body time   76f., 90–1
  consciousness in   74, 75
    mapping from   77–81
  cultural factors on   77
  dominance   74
  language for   77–8
  personalized   77–81
  regimented   74
    and flexible   76f.
  time-related goals   87
time-management   8, 55, 80
  disparities   78–9
  incubation periods with   82
  levels of thinking on   94–5
  pacing in   144–5
  personalized   74–5, 77, 93
  from prime time   90–1
  from prioritization   83–6f.
  on procrastination   82–3
  scope   93
  for work-life balance   90–3
trust   163–5
Tuckman, B. W.   157–8f.
Turnbull, J.   33n.   3

understanding 90, 124–5
    attainment and 172
    personalized 27–30
    in systems thinking 173
union initiatives 181–2
United Nations 137–8f.
urgency, importance and 84–6f.

values, beliefs and 22–3, 59
    as assertiveness keys 139
    as logical levels 186
    as neuro-logical levels 24–5f.,
        94–5
visual, auditory, kinaesthetic styles
        28, 29–30, 31–2, 33n. 16,
        109f., 122, 123–4f., 193–4
    anchoring from 49, 50–1
visual recall 123–4f.
voice 41, 105–6f.

Wales education system 187n. 8
well-being 69
work-life
    balance in 55–6
    from energy renewal 91–3
    from stability-zones 91–3
    from understanding 90
    disparities 18
    dominance 19–20
    paths 166–7
    personal skills and 5–6
    scope 55
    see also individual terms
workloads 83, 166–7
worry 63
worth 148–9
writing 63–5

yips 38f.